WILDLIFE

TREES

AND NONFLOWERING

PLANTS

Reader's Digest

The Reader's Digest Association, Inc.
Pleasantville, New York/Montreal

A READER'S DIGEST BOOK

Edited and designed by Media Projects Incorporated

Editors:
Edward S. Barnard
Sharon Fass Yates

Managing Editor:
Lelia Mander

Assistant Editor:
Aaron Murray

Production Manager:
Laura Smyth

Design:
Design Oasis

Copy Editor:
Charlotte Maurer

Consultant for revised edition:
Robert E. Budliger
Dir. of Environmental
Education (retired)
NY State Department of
Environmental Conservation

The credits and acknowledgments that appear on page 276 are hereby made a part of this copyright page.

Library of Congress Cataloging in Publication Data
Trees and nonflowering plants.
    p. cm. (North American Wildlife)
    Includes Index.
    ISBN 0-7621-0037-0
    1. Trees—North America—Identification. 2. Gymnosperms—
North America—Identification. 3. Fungi—North America—
Identification. 4. Cryptogams—Identification. I. Reader's Digest
Association.
QK110.N864   1998
582.16'.097—dc21   97-32725

This book contains revised material originally published in 1982 in the Reader's Digest book, NORTH AMERICAN WILDLIFE.

Reader's Digest and the Pegasus logo are registered trademarks of The Reader's Digest Association, Inc.

Printed in the United States of America
Second Printing, April 2000

NORTH AMERICAN WILDLIFE

TREES

AND NONFLOWERING

PLANTS

READER'S DIGEST

NORTH AMERICAN

CONTENTS

ABOUT THIS BOOK   6

TREES AND SHRUBS   8

NONFLOWERING PLANTS   132

MUSHROOMS   198

INDEX   270

CREDITS   276

ABOUT THIS BOOK

TREES AND NONFLOWERING PLANTS is both a browsing book filled with interesting lore about trees and other plants as well as a guide to identifying plants quickly, easily, and accurately. Use it to discover which fern grows up to 6 feet in height, why mushrooms are often found near certain kinds of trees, and a host of other fascinating facts. Use it also to recognize and identify all sorts of species—for instance, the toadstools that appear so magically after a rain or the small white-flowered trees that bloom in early spring when other forest trees remain bare.

Exhaustive in its coverage, this book includes more than 450 trees, shrubs, and nonflowering plants—from tiny lichens and delicate mosses to the towering conifers of West Coast forests. But of course it doesn't include *all* the species of North American trees, shrubs, and nonflowering plants; no single book—not even a dozen books—could do that. Instead, it features the most common, conspicuous, or important species—those that most people are likely to be curious about.

Each of the book's three sections starts with an introduction that explains how the section is organized and provides general identification tips. The entry for each species presents the identification information in an easy-to-find format. All you need to know to identify a species— size, special characteristics, habitat—is in a compact **identification capsule** separate from the text. The identification capsules supplement the color portraits of the species. Check marks on the art call your attention to certain features mentioned in the capsules. These **idento-checks** point out distinguishing details to look for when you're identifying a species.

Throughout TREES AND NONFLOWERING PLANTS there are some species, such as Giant Puffballs, that can be easily recognized by their appearance alone. Where you find these plants doesn't much matter (for identification purposes, at least). For others, where you find them is often an important clue to what they are. Finding any species is made easier by the **range map** that is a part of every entry. More convenient to use than lengthy written descriptions, these maps show where a species is likely to be. But since plants travel as seeds and spores, the ranges shown on the maps are approximations only. To attain pinpoint accuracy, you need to take into account the other information presented in the identification capsules.

HELPFUL IDENTIFICATION FEATURES

Idento-checks call your attention to certain features of the plant covered in the identification capsules.

Titles provide **common names** and are always followed by **scientific names.**

Easy-to-locate **identification capsules** contain the facts most important for identification.

Text blocks are packed with interesting lore and information about the plant.

Additional illustration boxes highlight details of many species—bark, flowers, fruits, leaf structure, spore cases, gills, or pores.

Range maps show at a glance where the plants reproduce without cultivation.

Basswoods *Tilia*

The basswoods, or lindens, supply welcome shade on city streets. Their soft, light-colored wood is a carver's delight. And their pale, fragrant flowers yield nectar that bees transform into a most flavorsome honey. All three North American species have heart-shaped leaves and straplike bracts.

American Basswood
Tilia americana

SIZE:
70-80 ft. tall; leaves 5-6 in. long.

WHAT TO LOOK FOR:
straplike bracts with hanging flowers or nutlets; leaves heart-shaped, coarsely toothed, smooth on both surfaces.

HABITAT:
bottomlands in damp loam.

BRACT WITH FRUIT

Cereuses *Cereus*

Highly resistant to drought, the 200-odd species in this group have a thick, rubbery "skin," spongy, water-storing tissues, and moisture-conserving needles instead of leaves. The only common North American tree in the group is the Saguaro.

Saguaro
(Giant Cactus)
Cereus giganteus

SIZE:
50-60 ft. tall; spines 1½ in. long.

WHAT TO LOOK FOR:
leaves spinelike, in clusters; trunk and branches fluted, bright green; flowers white; fruits red.

HABITAT:
desert valleys, slopes, and rocky hills.

70 North American Wildlife

Willows *Salix*

Most willows share a scale on the bud, sep ous projections at the the Arctic, are contine four hundred is only a Weeping Willow from species. Willows never formed sandbars, they roots. Before the age c vested for basketmakin

Sandbar Willow
Salix exigua

SIZE:
10-25 ft. tall (often shr

WHAT TO LOOK FOR:
leaves narrowly lance-sh
stems gray-green, uprigh

HABITAT:
along watercourses on ne

TREES AND SHRUBS

North America has the world's tallest trees, the most massive trees, and the oldest trees. Nearly 60 kinds of oaks, some 35 pines, and more than a dozen maples are found here. Altogether, 750 species of trees grow wild north of Mexico.

Exactly how many kinds of trees there are in North America depends to a great extent on which plants are considered trees. One generally accepted definition of a tree is a woody plant with one erect stem (the trunk) reaching a height of at least 12 feet. Shrubs are shorter, with multiple stems springing directly from the ground.

Just as most people know instinctively what a tree is, so too are they aware that some trees have needles and others leaves. This is a useful starting point in tree identification, but one that requires refinement. Needles are actually leaves—long narrow ones that, like other leaves, contain chlorophyll, the green pigment required for photosynthesis. Trees with needles belong to the group of plants called conifers, which produce their seeds in cones. (Cedars, junipers, and other trees with scalelike leaves are also conifers.) Nearly all conifers are evergreen; that is, they are never totally without leaves.

Unlike most conifers, the majority of broad-leaved trees (such as maples and oaks) are deciduous in temperate regions, shedding their leaves before winter sets in.

Although certain pines and other species often grow in pure stands, trees are more frequently found in associations; that is, if one species is present, so are its "partners," which do well under similar conditions. Oaks and hickories make up an association in several Southern and Central states; junipers and pinyons, in arid parts of the West. Similarly, certain understory plants are characteristic of one type of forest. Vine Maple grows in the shade of Northwestern conifers; Hobblebush, in mixed Northeastern forests.

Such associations extend to birds and other animal life. Sapsuckers tap out holes in birch trees; Red Crossbills eat the seeds of various conifers. Relationships like these point out an additional benefit of sharpening your skills in tree identification: if you know which trees are in the vicinity, you can predict what other forms of wildlife are likely to be nearby.

WHERE THE FORESTS ARE

North America has seven major types of forests, according to one widely accepted method of classification. The tree species listed below are typical members of their community.

Northern Forest:
Black Spruce, Tamarack, Balsam Fir, Paper Birch, Quaking Aspen

Pacific Coast Forest:
Western Hemlock, Redwood, Douglas-fir, Western Redcedar

Western Mountain Forest:
Ponderosa Pine, Lodgepole Pine, Englemann Spruce, Douglas-fir

Northeastern Forest:
Eastern Hemlock, American Beech, Northern Red Oak, American Basswood, Sugar Maple

Southeastern Forest:
Loblolly Pine, Shortleaf Pine, Longleaf Pine, Mockernut Hickory, Live Oak

Subropical Forest:
Red Mangrove, Black-mangrove, Cabbage Palmetto

Unforested Areas:
desert, grassland, tundra

Central Forest:
Tuliptree, Sycamore, Shagbark Hickory, White Oak, Ohio Buckeye

This section is divided into two parts. Species that usually grow as trees are covered on pages 12 through 108, with conifers preceding broad-leaved trees. Shrubs are on pages 109 through 131.

The measurements provided are for average-size, mature (fruiting) plants. Most leaves and twigs are pictured at one-quarter actual size. Exceptions include compound leaves, usually shown at one-eighth.

Tips for Identifying Trees

Certain species—Giant Sequoias, Weeping Willows—-can be recognized at a glance. Identifying others is a matter of narrowing down the possibilities.

Boxelder

Leaves. First determine the general type of leaf—needle-like, scalelike, or flat and broad. Then look at the size, shape, color, and arrangement. Most broad-leaved trees have alternating leaves. Some trees, such as boxelders, have compound leaves divided into leaflets.

Flowers. Large showy blossoms, such as those of magnolias, often lead to precise identification of a tree. Unflowerlike blossoms, such as birch catkins, can tell you to which group a particular tree belongs.

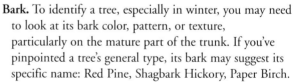

Pitch Pine

Fruits. Tree fruits can help you identify trees. Oak fruits (acorns) differ in size, shape, and texture depending upon their species. Conifer fruits (cones) are also quite varied. Check details and sizes of cones on the ground; also look at their orientation on branches.

Bark. To identify a tree, especially in winter, you may need to look at its bark color, pattern, or texture, particularly on the mature part of the trunk. If you've pinpointed a tree's general type, its bark may suggest its specific name: Red Pine, Shagbark Hickory, Paper Birch.

Ponderosa Pine

Shape. To determine a tree's shape, you must consider its height, crown width, arrangement of branches, and other characteristics. Shape varies with location. A forest tree, for example, will be taller and its crown narrower than the same species growing out in the open.

Identifying needle-leaved trees.

The chart below is a guide to conifers with needlelike leaves.
Conifers with short, scalelike leaves are shown on pages 32, 35-39.

Needle Arrangement	Needle Length	Needle in Cross Section	Tree Group
clusters of 5 (pinyons with fewer)	1-5 in.	usually triangular	white pines pp. 14-17
clusters of 2-4	1-18 in.	semicircular to triangular	yellow pines pp. 18-23
brushlike clusters of 20 or more	up to 2 in.	flat to triangular	larches p. 24
single, appearing to be on sides of branch	½-1 in.	flat	yews p. 13
single, all around branch	up to 2 in.	square or flattened	spruces pp. 25-28
single, on sides of branch or all around	up to 1 in.	flat	hemlocks p. 12
single, on top and sides of branch	up to 3 in.	flattened	true firs p. 29-30
	up to 1½ in.	flattened	Douglas-firs p. 31
single, on side of branch	up to 1 in.	flat	redwoods, baldcypresses p. 33-34

Hemlocks *Tsuga*

The long-lived hemlocks develop slowly in the shade of their forest companions, but in maturity produce such dense shade that few other species can grow beneath the graceful boughs. In the 19th century great forests of Eastern Hemlock were destroyed for the tannin in their bark, but now some of the forests are developing anew. Western Hemlock (*Tsuga heterophylla*) has longer cones and thrives on cool, moist slopes. The Carolina and Mountain hemlocks (*Tsuga caroliniana* and *mertensiana*), species of eastern and western mountains, respectively, have still longer cones.

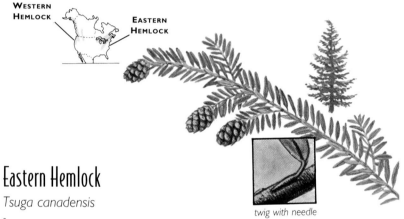

WESTERN HEMLOCK

EASTERN HEMLOCK

twig with needle

Eastern Hemlock

Tsuga canadensis

SIZE:
60-70 ft. tall; needles ⅓-⅔ in. long.

WHAT TO LOOK FOR:
needles flat, dark green above, whitish below, with short stem; cones small, on tip of branch; crown tip bent away from prevailing wind.

HABITAT:
shady ravines and north-facing slopes in cool, moist soils.

Yews *Taxus*

Red berrylike fruits distinguish the yews from other conifers. Tolerant of shade, yews are often the only shrubs or low trees growing beneath a dense forest canopy. Canada Yew (*Taxus canadensis*), a low shrub, is heavily browsed by winter-feeding moose and deer; the succulent fruits of various species are favored by grouse. Once prized for archery and hunting bows, yews are valued today as ornamental plants, especially on the north sides of buildings.

Pacific Yew

Taxus brevifolia

SIZE:
20-40 ft. tall; needles 1 in. long.

WHAT TO LOOK FOR:
needles dark green above, pale yellow-green below, growing all around branch but appearing to be in 2 rows; fruits scarlet, fleshy; bark thin, scaly, purple-brown.

HABITAT:
moist soils near water.

Pines *Pinus*

Although pines tend to have a more southerly distribution than spruces and firs, their natural range includes all of North America except the extreme North and some parts of the Midwest. Thirty-six species are native to this continent. Certain ones, such as the Eastern White Pine and the shorter-needled Western White Pine (*Pinus monticola*), grow almost everywhere, from wet bogs to dry ridges. Even such species as the Monterey Pine (*Pinus radiata*), naturally restricted to a small area, flourish in other areas when cultivated in tree plantations.

Foresters classify the pines into two groups—the white, or soft, pines and the yellow, or hard, pines—according to the characteristics of the heartwood, the central portion of the trunk. Although the heartwood is not visible on a living tree, other differences between the two groups can be more readily observed. Needles on white pines usually grow in clusters of five; on yellow species, in clusters of two or three. Cones on most yellow pines have prickles; those on a white pine are prickleless, with the exception of the Bristlecone Pine, a tree famed for its longevity (some specimens are the oldest trees in North America). Except for the Jack Pine, the trees shown on pages 14 through 17 are white pines; the Jack Pine and the species on pages 18 through 23 are yellow pines.

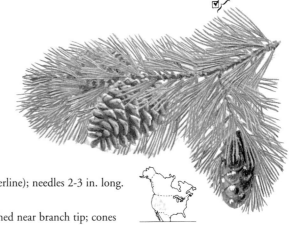

Limber Pine
Pinus flexilis

SIZE:
30-50 ft. tall (less at timberline); needles 2-3 in. long.

WHAT TO LOOK FOR:
needles in 5's, rigid, bunched near branch tip; cones green to brown, resinous; branches bend down but tips curve up.

HABITAT:
dry, rocky mountain slopes and peaks.

Sugar Pine

Pinus lambertiana

SIZE:
160-200 ft. tall; needles 2-4 in. long.

WHAT TO LOOK FOR:
needles in 5's, twisted; cones very long
(10-26 in.).

HABITAT:
cool, moist mountain slopes.

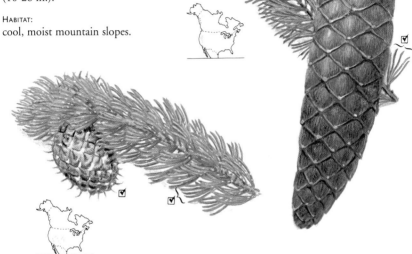

Bristlecone Pine

Pinus aristata

SIZE:
30-40 ft. tall (10 ft. at timberline);
needles 1-1½ in. long.

WHAT TO LOOK FOR:
needles in 5's, bright blue-green, with white
resin droplets; cone scales with sharp prickles.

HABITAT:
dry, rocky slopes to ridges.

ANCIENT BRISTLECONE PINES

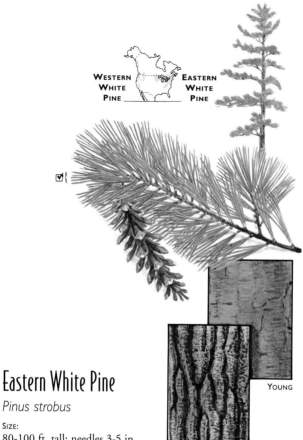

WESTERN
WHITE
PINE

EASTERN
WHITE
PINE

YOUNG

MATURE

Eastern White Pine

Pinus strobus

SIZE:
80-100 ft. tall; needles 3-5 in. long.

WHAT TO LOOK FOR:
needles in 5's; cones resinous; bark smooth, dark green (young) or deeply cracked, dark brown (mature).

HABITAT:
sandy loam, rock ridges, bogs.

Pinyon
Pinus edulis

SIZE:
20-40 ft. tall; needles ¾-1½ in. long.

WHAT TO LOOK FOR:
needles in 2's, dark green (Singleleaf Pinyon, *Pinus monophylla*, has solitary needles); cones egg-shaped; seeds wingless, ½ in. long.

HABITAT:
dry foothills, mesas, canyons.

Jack Pine
Pinus banksiana

SIZE:
30-70 ft. tall; needles ¾-1½ in. long.

WHAT TO LOOK FOR:
needles in 2's, curved, spread in V; cones usually closed, pointing toward branch tip; bark scaly, red-brown; tree often leaning or with distorted branches.

HABITAT:
dry, sandy plains to moist soils.

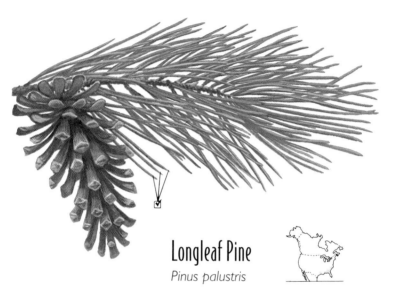

Longleaf Pine
Pinus palustris

SIZE:
80-120 ft. tall; needles 8-18 in. long.

WHAT TO LOOK FOR:
needles in 3's, bright green, densely bunched at branch tip; cones red-brown, large; bark orange-brown, with rough, scaly plates.

HABITAT:
deep, moist, sandy soils on ridges or knolls; poorly drained flats.

trees in "grass stage" (three to six years old) have almost no stems

Lodgepole Pine

Pinus contorta

SIZE:
70-80 ft. tall (shorter near sea); needles 1-3 in. long.

WHAT TO LOOK FOR:
needles in 2's, twisted; cones usually closed, prickly, pointing away from branch tip; bark with small plates (larger ones near sea).

HABITAT:
mountain slopes, beaches, bogs near sea.

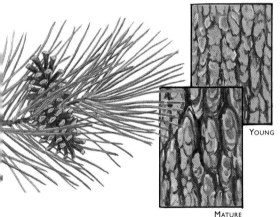

YOUNG

MATURE

Red Pine

(Norway Pine)

Pinus resinosa

SIZE:
50-80 ft. tall;
needles 4-6 in. long.

WHAT TO LOOK FOR:
needles in 2's, flexible, bunched near branch tips; cone scales without prickles; bark flaky, pink to red-brown (young) or with large, flat plates (mature).

HABITAT:
sandy soils, rocky slopes.

Shortleaf Pine

Pinus echinata

SIZE:
80-100 ft. tall; needles 2½-5 in. long.

WHAT TO LOOK FOR:
needles in 2's or 3's, dark green; cones with small prickles; bark almost black, scaly (young) or red-brown with large, flat plates (mature); young twigs green, with purplish tinge.

HABITAT:
sandy to dry, gravelly upland soils.

MATURE

Ponderosa Pine

(Western Yellow Pine)

Pinus ponderosa

SIZE:
150-180 ft. tall; needles 4-7 in. long.

WHAT TO LOOK FOR:
needles in 2's or 3's, dark yellow-green; cones with fine prickles; bark with large, flat plates overlaid with thin scales, brown to black (trees up to 100 years old) or yellow-brown (older).

HABITAT:
dry mountain soils.

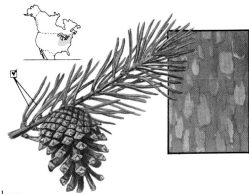

Scotch Pine
(Scots Pine)

Pinus sylvestris

SIZE:
50-60 ft. tall; needles 1½-3 in. long.

WHAT TO LOOK FOR:
needles in 2's, twisted, blue-green (yellow-green in winter);
bark bright orange, darkens with age.

HABITAT:
shelterbelts, tree plantations.

MALE   1   FEMALE   2   3

How pines reproduce

Pines, like other conifers, usually have two kinds of cones. In spring the
wind carries pollen from the short-lived male structures (often on the
lower branches) to the female cones (1). The female cones become
brown and woody as seeds ripen on the scales (2). The cones open and
release their seeds at maturity, usually in autumn of the second year (3).
Cones of some pines persist for several years and open as a result of fire.

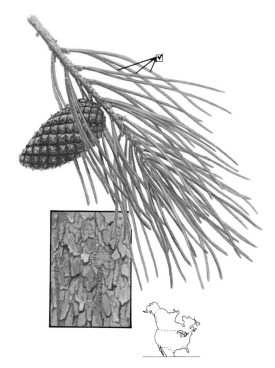

Slash Pine

Pinus elliottii

SIZE:
60-100 ft. tall; needles 7-10 in. long.

WHAT TO LOOK FOR:
needles in 2's or 3's, dark glossy green, bunched near branch tip;
cones lustrous, with stem and sharp prickles; bark purple-brown,
in plates with thin scales.

HABITAT:
moist, sandy soils; wet depressions.

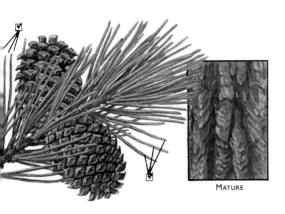

MATURE

Loblolly Pine

Pinus taeda

SIZE:
90-110 ft. tall; needles 6-9 in. long.

WHAT TO LOOK FOR:
needles in 3's, stiff, yellow-green; cones red-brown, with sharp triangular prickles; bark scaly, nearly black (young) or red-brown (mature); crown open, broad.

HABITAT:
sandy river bottoms and swamps to upland clay soils.

Pitch Pine

Pinus rigida

SIZE:
50-60 ft. tall; needles 3-5 in. long.

WHAT TO LOOK FOR:
needles in 3's, twisted, yellow-green, often in tufts on trunk; cones broad at base, with rigid prickles; bark in thick plates, often blackened by fire.

HABITAT:
sandy plains to rocky slopes.

Larches *Larix*

Unlike most conifers, larches turn yellow and shed their needles (but not their cones) in autumn. Of the three species native to cooler parts of North America, only the Western Larch (*Larix occidentalis*) is commercially important. The Subalpine Larch (*Larix lyallii*) is a timberline species.

WESTERN LARCH

Tamarack

(Eastern Larch)

Larix laricina

SIZE:
40-80 ft. tall; needles ¾-1½ in. long.

WHAT TO LOOK FOR:
needles bright blue-green, in dense clusters (except on new growth); cones yellow-brown, papery.

HABITAT:
swamps; bogs; upland forests in North.

Spruces *Picea*

Most of the world's 30 species of spruce share certain characteristics. Generally the needles are sharp and four-sided, and when crushed release a pungent odor. The woody base of the needle remains on the twig when the needle falls, making the twig feel rough to the touch. The mature cones hang down from the branch, in contrast with the erect cones of a fir. Each of the thin, papery scales making up the cone has two seeds, readily eaten by squirrels, crossbills, and other small mammals and birds.

Spruces are typically tall and conical, but soil and climate may alter their pattern of growth. In Alaska and northern Canada frost, wind, and a short growing season stunt the development of Black Spruce; trees more than a hundred years old may measure only 10 feet tall. In the southern Rockies, an Engelmann Spruce may hug the ground, its buds abraded by wind-borne particles.

Often associated in people's minds with northern forests, spruces penetrate south along mountain slopes. Two of the seven species native to North America—the Engelmann Spruce and the Blue Spruce (*Picea pungens*)—almost reach the Mexican border. (The Blue Spruce is also widely planted as an ornamental.) On eastern mountains the Red Spruce (*Picea rubens*) extends south to the Carolinas.

TWIG

Black Spruce

Picea mariana

SIZE:
30-40 ft. tall;
needles ¼-⅜ in. long.

WHAT TO LOOK FOR:
needles 4-sided, pale blue-green; twigs hairy; cones purple-brown, near top of tree.

HABITAT: bogs, swamps, lakeshores; bottomlands in Far North.

Norway Spruce

Picea abies

<small>SIZE:</small>
40-60 ft. tall; needles 1-1½ in. long.

<small>WHAT TO LOOK FOR:</small>
needles 4-sided but slightly flattened, dark yellow green; cones yellow-brown, with stiff, papery scales; twigs bright orange-brown; branches numerous, drooping (lower ones often touch ground); mature trees look shaggy.

<small>HABITAT:</small>
planted in gardens, shelterbelts, tree plantations; often around old farmhouses.

Engelmann Spruce

Picea engelmannii

SIZE:
100-120 ft. tall; needles 1 in. long.

WHAT TO LOOK FOR:
needles 4-sided, blue-green; cones light brown, with wavy edges on scales; bark with large, loose scales; lower branches drooping.

HABITAT:
high mountain slopes and meadows in moist soils.

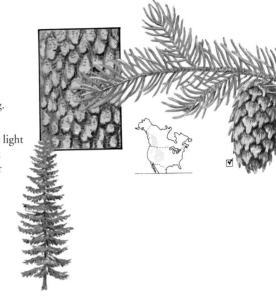

White Spruce

Picea glauca

SIZE:
60-70 ft. tall; needles ⅓-¾ in. long.

WHAT TO LOOK FOR:
needles 4-sided, blue-green, with waxy bloom; cones light brown; twigs hairless; bark on trunk with thin scales.

HABITAT:
streambanks, lakeshores, flats, slopes.

cross section
of needle

Sitka Spruce

Picea sitchensis

SIZE:
180-200 ft. tall; needles ½-1 in. long.

WHAT TO LOOK FOR:
needles flattened, bright yellow-green, sharp-tipped; cones flexible, with wavy edges on scales; bark reddish brown, loose, scaly; branches drooping.

HABITAT:
Pacific Coast rain forests in moist, loamy soils.

True Firs *Abies*

These graceful evergreens, worshipped by ancient Germanic tribes, were the inspiration for the Yuletide song "O Tannenbaum" ("O Christmas Tree"). Indeed, lights on a Christmas tree are thought to be imitations of the snow-covered cone stalks on a fir—the pencillike structures that remain near the tips of branches after the scales have fallen away from the cones. All 40 species of true firs (9 are native to North America) bear upright cones, in contrast with the hanging ones characteristic of most other conifers. True firs grow in cool, moist soils in northern lowland forests, reaching higher elevations farther to the south. The Fraser Fir (*Abies fraseri*) replaces the Balsam Fir in the southern Appalachians; in the West, the purple-coned Subalpine Fir (*Abies lasiocarpa*) grows south to New Mexico and Arizona.

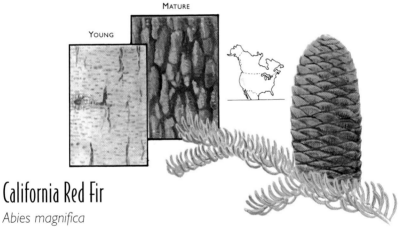

MATURE

YOUNG

California Red Fir
Abies magnifica

SIZE:
150-180 ft. tall; needles ¾-1½ in. long.

WHAT TO LOOK FOR:
needles flattened, silvery blue to dark green, curved upward; cones upright, purple-brown; bark smooth, whitish (young) or deeply furrowed and red-brown (mature).

HABITAT:
ravines, high mountain slopes.

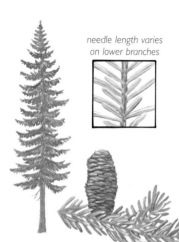

needle length varies on lower branches

Grand Fir
(Lowland White Fir)
Abies grandis

SIZE:
140-160 ft. tall; needles 1-2 in. long.

WHAT TO LOOK FOR:
needles flattened, dark shiny green above, silvery below, in 2 rows; branches bend down slightly but tips curve up.

HABITAT: stream valleys, gentle mountain slopes.

White Fir
Abies concolor

SIZE:
130-150 ft. tall; needles 2-3 in. long.

WHAT TO LOOK FOR:
needles flattened, silvery blue, turned up like hairbrush; cones upright, in top of tree; lower branches slant down.

HABITAT: high mountain slopes (usually north-facing) in well-drained soils.

Balsam Fir
Abies balsamea

SIZE: 40-60 ft. tall; needles ¾-1½ in. long.

WHAT TO LOOK FOR: needles flattened, dark shiny green, all around branch but appearing to be in 2 rows; cones upright, purple-green, resinous; bark dull green, smooth, with resin blisters.

CONE STALK

HABITAT: swamps to well-drained soils.

Douglas-firs *Pseudotsuga*

Rivaling the Redwood in height, the Douglas-fir grows tall and straight in moist coastal areas but occurs elsewhere in a very different form. Trees in the Rockies grow only about a third as tall, and their needles usually have a blue rather than a yellow cast. The *Douglas* in the name refers to David Douglas, a 19th-century botanical explorer.

Douglas-fir

Pseudotsuga menziesii

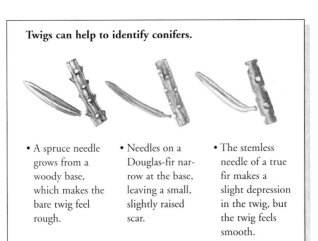

SIZE:
180-250 ft. tall;
needles ¾-1½ in. long.

WHAT TO LOOK FOR:
needles flat, yellow- or blue-green, all
around branch; cones hanging down, light brown,
with 3-pointed bract extending beyond scales.

HABITAT:
sea level to mountain slopes in moist, well-drained loam.

Twigs can help to identify conifers.

- A spruce needle grows from a woody base, which makes the bare twig feel rough.

- Needles on a Douglas-fir narrow at the base, leaving a small, slightly raised scar.

- The stemless needle of a true fir makes a slight depression in the twig, but the twig feels smooth.

Giant Sequoias *Sequoiadendron*

Although some sequoias are more than 3,000 years old, some Bristlecone Pines are still older. Redwoods are taller. But no trees grow more massive than the Giant Sequoias, or Bigtrees, which can measure more than 100 feet around at the base.

Giant Sequoia
Sequoiadendron giganteum

SIZE:
250-280 ft. tall;
leaves ⅛-½ in. long.

WHAT TO LOOK FOR:
huge tree with massive trunk; leaves blue-green, scalelike, overlapping (needlelike at branch tips); cones oval, reddish brown, with thick scales.

HABITAT:
western slopes of Sierra Nevada.

Redwoods *Sequoia*

Both Redwoods and Giant Sequoias are relics of the ancient past. Frequently confused in people's minds because of their impressive size, the two kinds of conifers are quite different in both appearance and habitat. Redwoods thrive in moist coastal areas, while the Giant Sequoias are associated with drier mountain areas.

Redwood

Sequoia sempervirens

SIZE:

200-300 ft. tall;
needles ½-1 in. long.

WHAT TO LOOK FOR:

needles dark yellow-green, in 2 rows (scalelike on cone-bearing twigs and tips of new growth).

HABITAT:

moist streambanks and slopes in Pacific Coast fog belt.

Baldcypresses *Taxodium*

Typically festooned with Spanish Moss, the Baldcypress has "knees" arising from the root system. Their function remains a matter of speculation. The tree is unusual in habit as well as appearance; though a conifer, it sheds its leaves in autumn. Its close relative, the Montezuma Baldcypress (*Taxodium mucronatum*), is evergreen.

Baldcypress

Taxodium distichum

SIZE:
100-120 ft. tall;
needles ½-¾ in. long.

WHAT TO LOOK FOR:
needles in 2 rows, flat, yellow-green (summer) or red-brown (fall); trunk broad at base, often surrounded by bark-covered "knees."

HABITAT:
swamps to seasonally flooded bottomlands.

Thujas *Thuja*

Sometimes called arborvitae ("tree of life"), thujas are known to live for several hundred years, their lacy boughs and scalelike foliage supplying deer with shelter and browse. Both North American species, as well as their Oriental relatives, are widely cultivated as ornamentals. Northern White-cedar supplies lumber for fences, rustic furniture, and planking for small boats; Western Redcedar, shingles and siding.

Western Redcedar
(Giant Arborvitae)
Thuja plicata

SIZE:
150-200 ft. tall; leaves about 1 in. long.

WHAT TO LOOK FOR:
leaves scalelike, overlapping, shiny, dark yellow-green, in drooping fernlike sprays; cones light brown, with opposing leathery scales.

HABITAT:
moist flats and slopes, riverbanks, bogs, swamps.

Northern White-cedar
(Eastern Arborvitae)
Thuja occidentalis

SIZE:
40-50 ft. tall; leaves ⅛-¼ in. long.

WHAT TO LOOK FOR:
leaves scalelike, overlapping, dull green, in flat fanlike sprays, with raised resin glands on underside; cones tan, with opposing woody scales.

HABITAT:
limestone bluffs and outcrops; fields, bogs, swamps.

White-cedars *Chamaecyparis*

As the qualifying adjective "white" suggests, these trees are not considered true cedars. (True cedars, closely related to the pines, are not native to North America.) White-cedars are also called false cypresses—an example of the confusing nomenclature within the cypress family, which includes all the trees on this page and on pages 35, 37, 38, and 39.

Atlantic White-cedar

(Southern White-cedar) *Chamaecyparis thyoides*

SIZE:
80-85 ft. tall; leaves about ⅛ in. long.

WHAT TO LOOK FOR:
leaves scalelike, overlapping, dark blue-green, with raised resin glands; cones round, bluish purple with waxy bloom; bark gray, with narrow, flat-topped ridges.

HABITAT:
peat swamps, bogs.

Port-Orford-cedar

(Lawson Cypress)

Chamaecyparis lawsoniana

SIZE:
140-180 ft. tall; leaves ¹⁄₁₆ in. long.

WHAT TO LOOK FOR:
leaves overlapping, scalelike, bright yellow- to blue-green; branches lacy, pendulous; cones red-brown, with waxy bloom.

HABITAT:
moist valleys and slopes to dry ridges.

Cypresses *Cupressus*

In southern California and other arid regions of the West, seven species of this drought-resistant group endure fires, parched soil, and, in some cases, saltwater spray. Their leaves are tiny, coated with wax, and composed of thickened cells with sunken stomates (breathing pores)—all adaptations to a dry environment.

Arizona Cypress

Cupressus arizonica

SIZE:
50-60 ft. tall; leaves ⅟₁₆ in. long.

WHAT TO LOOK FOR:
leaves overlapping, scalelike, pale blue-green; cones round, reddish brown, with 6 or 8 pointed scales.

HABITAT:
canyons and mountain slopes in moist to dry soils.

Monterey Cypress

Cupressus macrocarpa

SIZE:
60-70 ft. tall; leaves ⅟₁₆ in. long.

WHAT TO LOOK FOR:
leaves overlapping, scalelike, dark green; cones round, dark brown; young tree straight; old tree usually contorted, with branches as long as trunk.

HABITAT:
windswept sandy to rocky shores near Monterey, California.

Junipers *Juniperus*

Junipers are a diverse group, as their shapes and sizes suggest; the 13 North American species range from the ground-hugging Creeping Juniper (*Juniperus horizontalis*) to the pyramidal Eastern Redcedar. Capable of growing almost anywhere except in wet soil, junipers often thrive in areas where other trees cannot grow or have not yet become established. Such species as the Utah Juniper and the Oneseed Juniper (*Juniperus monosperma*) supply welcome visual relief on dry western slopes; the Eastern Redcedar and Common Juniper invade abandoned fields and serve as pioneers, creating an environment hospitable to the growth of broad-leaved trees. Cedar chests are made from the fragrant wood of the Eastern Redcedar; the "berries" (technically considered cones) of the Common Juniper are used as flavoring in gin.

Common Juniper
(Dwarf Juniper)
Juniperus communis

SIZE:
1-3 ft. tall; leaves ⅓ in. long.

WHAT TO LOOK FOR:
leaves in whorls of 3, needlelike, whitish above; fruits berrylike, dark blue, with whitish powder; occasionally tree-size, but usually a sprawling shrub.

HABITAT:
abandoned fields; sandy to rocky flats and slopes.

Eastern Redcedar

Juniperus virginiana

YOUNG
FOLIAGE

MATURE
FOLIAGE

SIZE:
40-50 ft. tall; leaves
⅟₁₆-¼ in. long.

WHAT TO LOOK FOR:
leaves overlapping,
dark green, scalelike
(mature) or needlelike (young);
cones berrylike, dark blue, with
waxy bloom; crown may be narrowly or broadly pyramidal.

HABITAT:
abandoned fields with poor, dry soils.

Utah Juniper

(Bigberry Juniper)

Juniperus osteosperma

SIZE:
10-30 ft. tall; leaves ⅟₁₆ in. long.

WHAT TO LOOK FOR:
leaves overlapping, scalelike, yellow-green, on stout
twigs; cones berrylike, brownish, with waxy
bloom; trunk short, often with many branches.

HABITAT:
flats, slopes, mesas with poor, dry soils.

Ginkgoes *Ginkgo*

Fossils reveal that many different kinds of ginkgoes existed in the geological past. Today only one species remains, and it too might have become extinct had it not been planted in the temple gardens of China and Japan. Native to the Orient, the Ginkgo is a popular ornamental tree because of its resistance to insects, disease, and pollution.

Ginkgo

(Maidenhair Tree)

Ginkgo biloba

SIZE:
30-50 ft. tall; leaves 2-3 in. wide.

WHAT TO LOOK FOR:
leaves fan-shaped, leathery, yellow to dark green, with veins fanning from narrow end; fruits fleshy, yellow.

HABITAT: city streets and parks.

Asiminas *Asimina*

Large fleshy fruits, showy flowers, and pungent leaves and twigs characterize the asiminas. They belong to the chiefly tropical custard-apple family, whose name aptly describes the fruit of the Pawpaw. The other seven native asiminas are low shrubs or small trees that grow in the shade of taller hardwoods, mostly in the Southeast and Gulf Coast.

Pawpaw

Asimina triloba

SIZE:
10-30 ft. tall; leaves 5-10 in. long.

WHAT TO LOOK FOR:
leaves narrow at base, widest at mid-point; flowers with 6 purplish petals; fruits fleshy, greenish yellow to brown; tree may be shrubby.

HABITAT:
bottomlands in rich, moist soil.

Yellow-poplars *Liriodendron*

The Tuliptree is one of the tallest, straightest eastern broad-leaved trees, and its trunk is among the largest in diameter. Its tulip-shaped blossoms, borne high above the ground, are camouflaged by the green on the outer petals; only when the blossoms fall prematurely are the bright inner petals revealed. The tree has one living relative, the Chinese Tuliptree (*Liriodendron chinense*).

FRUIT

Tuliptree
(Yellow-poplar)
Liriodendron tulipifera

SIZE:
100-120 ft. tall; leaves 4-6 in. long.

WHAT TO LOOK FOR:
leaves 4-lobed, with deeply notched tip, shiny, bright green; flowers tuliplike, green and orange; fruits cone-like, tan, remaining on tree after leaves drop.

HABITAT:
moist but well-drained sandy to stony loam.

Sassafrases *Sassafras*

The one North American tree in this group (often a shrub in the North) has aromatic twigs and leaves. The root bark makes a spicy tea, once imbibed as a tonic. Bees favor the nectar of the blossoms, and birds the glossy fruits.

Sassafras
Sassafras albidum

SIZE:
30-40 ft. tall; leaves 3-5 in. long.

WHAT TO LOOK FOR:
leaves oval, 3-lobed, or mitten-shaped; twigs bright green, aromatic when crushed; fruits blue, berrylike; stump and roots sprout readily.

HABITAT:
well-drained old fields and woods; often in hedgerows.

California-laurels *Umbellularia*

A large tree in Oregon, the single species in this group is a low-growing shrub in southern California, where it is flattened by wind and salt spray. Like other members of the aromatic laurel family, including Sassafras and Spicebush, it produces highly volatile oils with a pleasing odor.

California-laurel
(Oregon-myrtle) *Umbellularia californica*

SIZE:
40-80 ft. tall; leaves 2-5 in. long.

WHAT TO LOOK FOR:
leaves elliptical, evergreen, with odor of camphor when crushed; fruits yellow-green.

HABITAT:
rich bottomlands to dry rocky slopes and bluffs.

Sweetgums *Liquidambar*

Oozing from wounds in the trunk of a Sweetgum is a fragrant but bitter-tasting resin, used in times past as a chewing gum and a treatment for skin disorders and dysentery. The leaves of the single North American species yield a pleasant odor when crushed, and they turn a spectacular red in fall. Although they might be mistaken for maple leaves, they do not grow in pairs.

TWIG

Sweetgum

(Redgum)

Liquidambar styraciflua

SIZE:
80-120 ft. tall; leaves 6-7 in. wide.

WHAT TO LOOK FOR:
leaves star-shaped, with 5-7 points; fruits round, woody, with stout spines, remaining on tree in winter; twigs with corky projections.

HABITAT:
rich bottomlands, swamps.

Magnolias *Magnolia*

Magnolialike fossils more than 70 million years old indicate the ancient lineage of these beautiful trees. In fact, one major classification system for plants is based on the premise that magnolias were the ancestors of all other flowering plants.

According to this theory, they were the first plants to bear seeds in a protective ovary, or fruit (pine and other conifer seeds are "naked"). Magnolias cultivated for their pinkish blossoms in early spring are a hybrid of two Chinese species.

Southern Magnolia

(Evergreen Magnolia) *Magnolia grandiflora*

SIZE:
60-80 ft. tall; leaves 5-8 in. long.

WHAT TO LOOK FOR:
leaves oval, leathery, evergreen, with dense rusty hairs on underside; flowers large, fragrant, with 6-12 white petals.

HABITAT:
rich, well-drained bottomlands.

underside of leaf

Sweetbay

(Swamp Magnolia)
Magnolia virginiana

SIZE:
40-60 ft. tall; leaves 3-5 in. long.

WHAT TO LOOK FOR:
leaves elliptical, shiny bright green above, whitish below, persisting through winter in South; flowers creamy white.

HABITAT:
edges of swamps and moist lowlands on coastal plain.

Cucumbertree

(Cucumber Magnolia)
Magnolia acuminata

SIZE:
80-90 ft. tall; leaves 6-10 in. long.

WHAT TO LOOK FOR:
leaves broadly elliptical, pointed at tip, yellow-green above, light green below; flowers pale yellow-green; seeds red, hanging by slender threads from fruit.

HABITAT:
gentle slopes and stream valleys in moist, rich soil.

FRUIT

Hackberries *Celtis*

The Hackberry has one very conspicuous feature: distorted clusters of short twigs ("witches' brooms"), caused by mites that inject a growth-retarding substance into the leaf buds. The Sugarberry (*Celtis laevigata*), a tree of the Mississippi River valley and the Southeast, closely resembles the Hackberry except for its sweet reddish-orange or yellow fruit.

Hackberry
Celtis occidentalis

SIZE:
30-40 ft. tall; leaves 2½-4 in. long.

WHAT TO LOOK FOR:
leaves oval, toothed, with curved tip and lopsided base; bark gray, with corky ridges; fruits dark purple; clusters of distorted twigs near branch tips.

HABITAT:
rich bottomlands to limestone outcrops.

WITCHES'
BROOMS

Mulberries *Morus*

With fruits and leaves relished by man and silkworms respectively, these rapidly growing, drought-resistant trees have been transplanted around the world. Crusaders took the Black Mulberry (*Morus nigra*) from the eastern Mediterranean to the British Isles; the Pilgrims brought it to the New World, where it now reproduces in the wild. White Mulberry (*Morus alba*) is also an escape; Red Mulberry is a native tree. All are named for the commonest color of their fruit.

Red Mulberry

Morus rubra

SIZE:
20-30 ft. tall; leaves 3-5 in. long.

WHAT TO LOOK FOR:
leaves oval, mitten-shaped, or 3-lobed, coarsely toothed, hairy below; fruits dark red to purple.

HABITAT:
bottomlands and gentle slopes in rich, moist soil.

Elms *Ulmus*

In the 1920s a fungus believed to have originated in Asia (Asian species are resistant) killed millions of elms in northern Europe. Carried by bark beetles, Dutch elm disease struck eastern North America in the 1930s. Sweeping westward, it has affected all six native elms. The graceful, vase-shaped American Elm is the most widespread species. The other wide-ranging species, the Slippery Elm (*Ulmus rubra*), has a similar appearance when viewed from a distance, but its twigs and fruits are distinctly different.

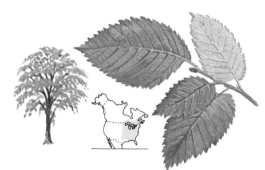

American Elm
(White Elm)

Ulmus americana

SIZE:
50-60 ft. tall; leaves 4-6 in. long.

WHAT TO LOOK FOR:
leaves broadly elliptical, with parallel veins and toothed edges; seed surrounded by thin, hairy collar notched at tip; twigs gray, with chestnut-brown buds (winter); crown arched, spreading.

HABITAT:
bottomlands to moist uplands.

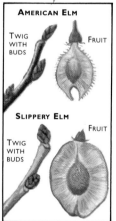

AMERICAN ELM

TWIG WITH BUDS

FRUIT

SLIPPERY ELM

TWIG WITH BUDS

FRUIT

Winged Elm
(Wahoo)

Ulmus alata

SIZE:
30-40 ft. tall; leaves 2 in. long.

WHAT TO LOOK FOR:
leaves elliptical, toothed, in 2 rows in same plane; twigs with corky projections (wings).

HABITAT:
dry, gravelly uplands to rich, moist bottomlands.

Osage-oranges *Maclura*

Native to the south-central states, the Osage-orange was widely planted in the 1930s as a shelterbelt and hedge tree, and now grows wild in many parts of the East. Many people consider it a pest because of its thorny twigs and messy (but attractive) fruit, which exudes a milky sap when bruised.

Osage-orange

Maclura pomifera

SIZE:
30-40 ft. tall; leaves 3-5 in. long.

WHAT TO LOOK FOR:
leaves broadly lance-shaped, shiny dark green above; stout spines on twigs; baseball-size fruits yellow-green, nubbly; bark furrowed, shreddy.

HABITAT:
rich bottomlands; planted in hedgerows and shelterbelts.

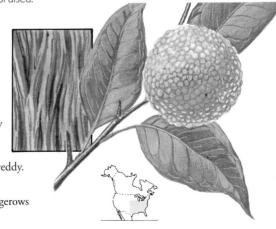

Sycamores *Platanus*

With their buttonball fruits and mottled bark, sycamores attract attention wherever they grow. In nature they usually prosper along a stream; for example, the California Sycamore (*Platanus racemosa*) thrives on mountain streambanks. But cities also have their sycamore—the London Planetree, a cross between the Sycamore and the Oriental Planetree (*Platanus orientalis*). The seed balls of the Sycamore hang singly from the twig; the London Plane's often occur in twos and threes; and the California Sycamore has up to seven on a threadlike stem.

Sycamore
(Planetree)

Platanus occidentalis

SIZE:
80-100 ft. tall;
leaves 4-7 in. wide.

WHAT TO LOOK FOR:
leaves wide, large-toothed, with 3-5 shallow lobes; fruits round, bristly; bark mottled, peeling in irregular flakes.

HABITAT:
bottomlands in rich, moist soil.

Walnuts *Juglans*

The delectable kernel of the Black Walnut is diabolically hard to extract. First the sturdy husk must be crushed (some people suggest driving over it with a car). Then the nut must be peeled, which is difficult to do without staining your hands (the husks furnish a substance used as a dye). The rocklike inner shell yields only to repeated hammerblows. Store-bought walnuts—from the English Walnut (*Juglans regia*)—are easier to crack, and their typically thick, semi-fleshy husks are removed before the nuts are shipped.

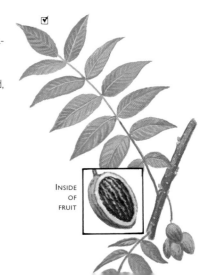

INSIDE
OF
FRUIT

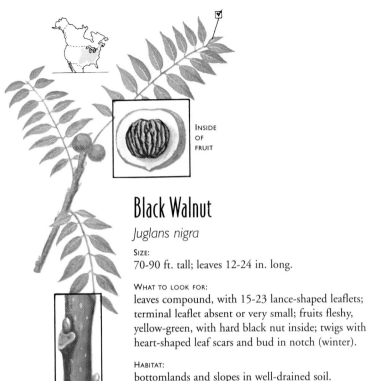

INSIDE OF FRUIT

TWIG

Black Walnut

Juglans nigra

SIZE:
70-90 ft. tall; leaves 12-24 in. long.

WHAT TO LOOK FOR:
leaves compound, with 15-23 lance-shaped leaflets; terminal leaflet absent or very small; fruits fleshy, yellow-green, with hard black nut inside; twigs with heart-shaped leaf scars and bud in notch (winter).

HABITAT:
bottomlands and slopes in well-drained soil.

◄Butternut

(White Walnut)

Juglans cinerea

SIZE:
40-60 ft. tall; leaves 15-30 in. long.

WHAT TO LOOK FOR:
leaves compound, with 11-17 lance-shaped leaflets and hairy stem; terminal leaflet full size; fruits sticky, yellow-green.

HABITAT:
moist ravines and gentle slopes to dry rocky hillsides.

Hickories *Carya*

Close relatives of the walnuts, hickories have fewer leaflets per leaf, slimmer twigs, catkins hanging three from a stem, and husks that split in four sections when the nuts are ripe. (Walnut catkins are single or in pairs; the fruit husks do not split at maturity.) Hickory nuts are smooth (sometimes with four or six ribs) and generally edible, although some are bitter and others so small as to be hardly worth the trouble of cracking. In the wild, the various kinds of hickory hybridize quite freely, resulting in a wide variety of growth forms that challenge even the expert at identification. Hickory wood is tough, making excellent tool handles and firewood.

Bitternut Hickory

Carya cordiformis

TWIG WITH BUDS

FRUIT

SIZE:
50-60 ft. tall; leaves 7-13 in. long.

WHAT TO LOOK FOR:
leaves compound, with 7-11 leaflets, in pairs gradually decreasing in size from apex; buds yellow, hairy; fruits with thin, scaly husks splitting part way into 4 sections, and gray or red-brown bitter-tasting nuts.

HABITAT:
bottomlands with well-drained soil; streambanks, swamps, dry uplands.

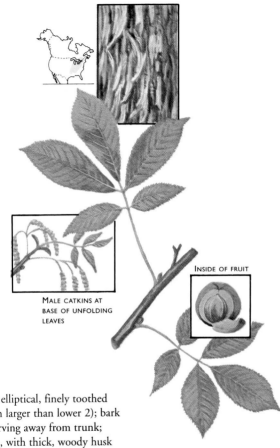

Shagbark Hickory

Carya ovata

MALE CATKINS AT
BASE OF UNFOLDING
LEAVES

INSIDE OF FRUIT

SIZE:
70-80 ft. tall;
leaves 10-14 in. long.

WHAT TO LOOK FOR:
leaves compound, with 5 elliptical, finely toothed
leaflets (upper 3 are much larger than lower 2); bark
with long, loose strips curving away from trunk;
fruits nearly round, green, with thick, woody husk
and thin-shelled nut.

HABITAT:
moist bottomlands to upland slopes.

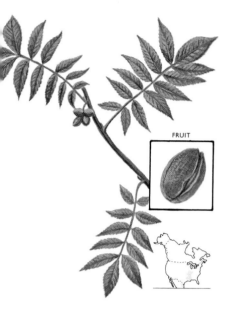

Pecan

Carya illinoensis

SIZE:
110-140 ft. tall;
leaves 12-20 in. long.

WHAT TO LOOK FOR:
leaves compound, with 9-17 broadly lance-shaped, finely toothed leaflets; nuts in clusters of 3-12, dark brown, surrounded by thin husks that split in 4.

HABITAT:
bottomlands in rich, well-drained soil.

FRUIT

Mockernut Hickory

Carya tomentosa

SIZE:
40-60 ft. tall; leaves 9-14 in. long.

WHAT TO LOOK FOR:
leaves compound, with 7-9 finely toothed leaflets, densely haired below; fruits nearly round, with thick brown husk and small nuts.

HABITAT:
moist uplands to dry, sandy slopes and ridges.

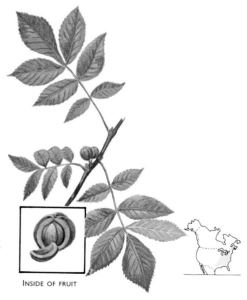

INSIDE OF FRUIT

Tanoaks *Lithocarpus*

Although tanoaks have oaklike leaves and fruits, their blossoms resemble those of chestnuts and chinkapins (the flower clusters are upright rather than hanging). The single North American species was formerly used as a source of tannin.

Tanoak

Lithocarpus densiflorus

SIZE:
70-90 ft. tall; leaves 3-5 in. long.

WHAT TO LOOK FOR:
leaves evergreen, leathery, rusty below (turning white toward fall), sometimes with widely spaced teeth; acorn with hairy cup.

HABITAT:
bottomlands to gentle slopes in moist soil.

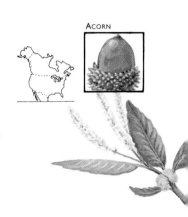

ACORN

Beeches *Fagus*

Patriarch of the eastern hardwood forest, the American Beech is the only North American plant in this primarily Eurasian group, whose thin gray bark and papery leaves are unmistakable. A peculiarity of this tree is that the dead leaves may stay on it all winter, twisting and rustling in the wind.

American Beech

Fagus grandifolia

SIZE:
70-80 ft. tall; leaves 2½-5 in. long.

WHAT TO LOOK FOR:
leaves elliptical with sharp, widely spaced teeth, bark smooth, light gray; fruits with spiny husk and 2-3 triangular nuts; buds long, slender.

HABITAT:
bottomlands and gentle slopes.

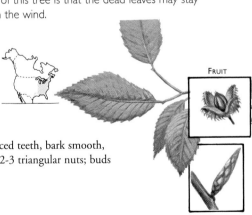

FRUIT

BUD

Chinkapins *Castanopsis*

The Giant Chinkapin is only occasionally giant-size (it is a shrub in Washington); the Sierra Chinkapin (*Castanopsis sempervirens*) is a low-growing timberline species. Neither should be confused with the Allegheny Chinkapin, which is a chestnut.

Giant Chinkapin
Castanopsis chrysophylla

SIZE:
60-80 ft. tall; leaves 2-6 in. long.

WHAT TO LOOK FOR:
leaves lance-shaped, evergreen, leathery, yellow below, with edges rolled under; fruits spiny, with 1-2 nuts.

HABITAT:
moist valleys to dry slopes.

Allegheny Chinkapin
Castanea pumila

SIZE:
5-15 ft. tall; leaves 3-5 in. long.

WHAT TO LOOK FOR:
leaves elliptical, whitish and hairy below, with widely spaced bristle-tipped teeth; fruits spiny, with single nut.

HABITAT:
dry woods and thickets.

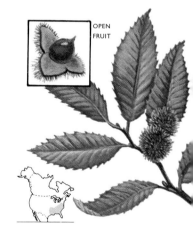

OPEN FRUIT

Chestnuts *Castanea*

Today's chestnuts roasting on an open fire are from Spanish Chestnut trees (*Castanea sativa*). The once common American Chestnut was virtually exterminated by a fungus blight, which is believed to have been brought from Asia about 1900. Although sprouts still develop from tree stumps, nearly all die before bearing fruit.

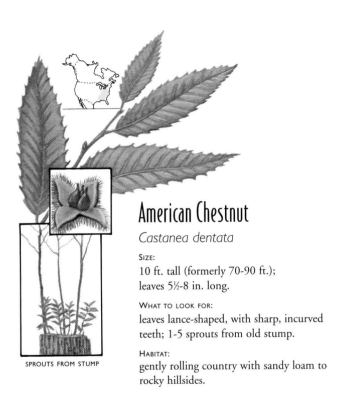

SPROUTS FROM STUMP

American Chestnut
Castanea dentata

SIZE:
10 ft. tall (formerly 70-90 ft.);
leaves 5½-8 in. long.

WHAT TO LOOK FOR:
leaves lance-shaped, with sharp, incurved teeth; 1-5 sprouts from old stump.

HABITAT:
gently rolling country with sandy loam to rocky hillsides.

Oaks *Quercus*

Of all the broad-leaved trees in North America, oaks are the most widespread, occupy the greatest variety of habitats, and comprise the largest number of species (58 trees and 10 shrubs). The leaves on a single tree may come in many shapes, and the species hybridize freely, adding to the complexity of identification. Pinpointing the species of oak is easiest if the tree is first classified into one of two groups—the red oaks (pages 58-62) or the white oaks (pages 63-65). Red oaks bear tiny bristles at the tip of the leaf, at the ends of the lobes, or both. Their bitter acorns require two years to mature (they therefore remain on the trees in winter), and woolly hairs line the cup. The leaves of white oaks have rounded lobes devoid of bristles. Their sweet acorns mature in six months (and are gone by winter), and the inner wall of the cup is smooth.

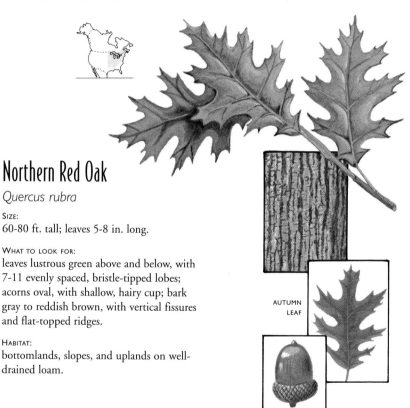

Northern Red Oak

Quercus rubra

SIZE:
60-80 ft. tall; leaves 5-8 in. long.

WHAT TO LOOK FOR:
leaves lustrous green above and below, with 7-11 evenly spaced, bristle-tipped lobes; acorns oval, with shallow, hairy cup; bark gray to reddish brown, with vertical fissures and flat-topped ridges.

HABITAT:
bottomlands, slopes, and uplands on well-drained loam.

AUTUMN LEAF

ACORN

Individual species of oak can be identified by their leaves (shape and sometimes color) and fruits, or acorns. The acorns are shown here life-size. In winter, when little other food is available, acorns are a staple in the diet of many birds and mammals—among others, ducks, grouse, quail, turkeys, jays, titmice, woodpeckers, bears, raccoons, squirrels, and deer. Such animals may help propagate oaks by dispersing, storing, and then never reclaiming the acorns. A sprouting acorn develops full-sized leaves and unusually long roots, giving the seedling an advantage in the race toward maturity.

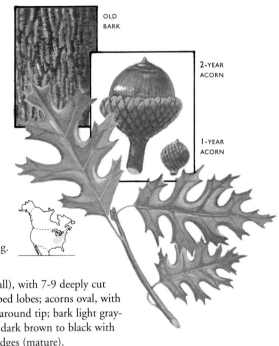

OLD
BARK

2-YEAR
ACORN

1-YEAR
ACORN

Scarlet Oak

Quercus coccinea

SIZE:
70-80 ft. tall; leaves 3-6 in. long.

WHAT TO LOOK FOR:
leaves bright green (scarlet in fall), with 7-9 deeply cut (almost to midvein) bristle-tipped lobes; acorns oval, with deep cup and concentric rings around tip; bark light gray-brown and smooth (young) or dark brown to black with shallow fissures and irregular ridges (mature).

HABITAT:
dry sandy to gravelly soils.

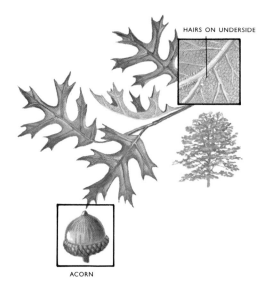

HAIRS ON UNDERSIDE

ACORN

Pin Oak

(Swamp Oak)

Quercus palustris

Sɪᴢᴇ: 70-80 ft. tall; leaves 3-5 in. long.

Wʜᴀᴛ ᴛᴏ ʟᴏᴏᴋ ғᴏʀ: leaves 5-lobed (occasionally 7 or 9), deeply cut, bristle-tipped, with tufts of hair on underside; acorns round, with shallow cup; tree with many small branches and downward-hanging lower limbs.

Hᴀʙɪᴛᴀᴛ: wet bottomlands.

Coast Live Oak

Quercus agrifolia

Sɪᴢᴇ:
60-90 ft. tall; leaves ¾-3 in. long.

Wʜᴀᴛ ᴛᴏ ʟᴏᴏᴋ ғᴏʀ:
leaves evergreen, elliptical, leathery, with spiny teeth and edges that tend to roll under; acorns slender, with scaly cup.

Hᴀʙɪᴛᴀᴛ:
dry valleys, canyons; slopes.

ACORN

Blackjack Oak

(Barren Oak)

Quercus marilandica

SIZE:
20-30 ft. tall; leaves 3-7 in. long.

WHAT TO LOOK FOR:
leathery, wedge-shaped, 3-lobed leaves, with brownish to rusty hairs on underside; cup covers half of acorn.

HABITAT:
dry sandy flatlands to barren rocky slopes.

Willow Oak

(Peach Oak)

Quercus phellos

SIZE:
80-100 ft. tall; leaves 2-5 in. long.

WHAT TO LOOK FOR:
leaves narrowly lance-shaped, shiny light green above, gray-green below; acorns almost round, with thin cups.

HABITAT:
rich bottomlands; poorly drained flats; moist uplands.

Live Oak

Quercus virginiana

SIZE:
40-50 ft. tall; leaves 2-5 in. long.

WHAT TO LOOK FOR:
leaves elliptical, without lobes, semi-evergreen, leathery, glossy dark green above, pale green and hairy below; acorns shiny, dark brown (almost black); tree often wider than it is tall (shrubby near coast).

HABITAT:
coastal sand plains and dunes to inland sand flats in dry to wet soil.

ACORN

California Black Oak

Quercus kelloggii

SIZE:
50-60 ft. tall; leaves 4-10 in. long.

WHAT TO LOOK FOR:
leaves yellow-green, with 7 (occasionally 9) bristle-tipped lobes; acorns elongated, with deep cup.

HABITAT:
dry lower mountain slopes, canyons, and grasslands.

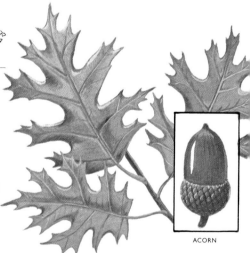

ACORN

ACORN

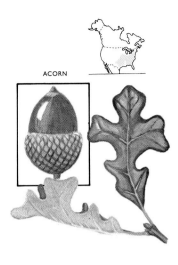

Post Oak

Quercus stellata

SIZE:
40-50 ft. tall; leaves 4-6 in. long.

WHAT TO LOOK FOR:
leaves broadly cross-shaped, leathery, dark green, with gray to yellow hairs on underside.

HABITAT:
dry sandy or gravelly uplands and plains; rocky ridges and hills; riverbanks in loam.

White Oak

Quercus alba

SIZE:
80-100 ft. tall; leaves 5-9 in. long.

WHAT TO LOOK FOR:
leaves bright green above, pale green below, with 7-9 rounded major lobes (clefts between lobes may be deep or shallow); acorn cup shallow, with knobby scales.

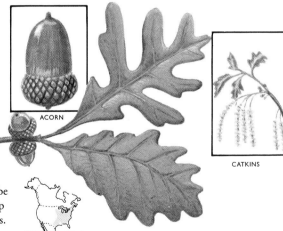

ACORN

CATKINS

HABITAT:
riverbanks; moist valleys to sandy plains and dry hillsides.

ACORN

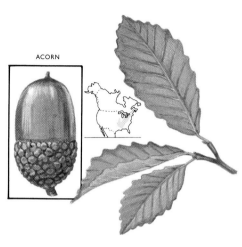

Chestnut Oak
(Rock Oak)
Quercus prinus

SIZE:
50-60 ft. tall; leaves 4-8 in. long.

WHAT TO LOOK FOR:
leaves elliptical, with 17-21 shallow lobes, lustrous yellow-green above, pale green and finely haired below; acorns shiny, with thin cup and long stem.

HABITAT:
dry sandy uplands to rocky ridges; valleys with well-drained soil.

Valley Oak
(California White Oak)
Quercus lobata

SIZE:
70-100 ft. tall; leaves 2½-4 in. long.

WHAT TO LOOK FOR:
leaves dark green above, gray-green and hairy below, with 7-11 rounded, deeply cut lobes; acorns long, tapering to point, with bowllike knobby cup; tree massive.

HABITAT:
rich valleys to dry gravelly hillsides.

ACORN

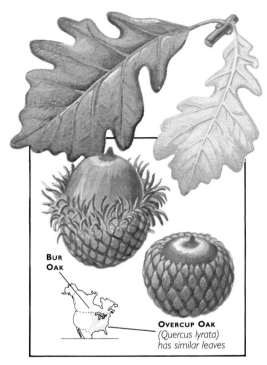

BUR OAK

OVERCUP OAK
(Quercus lyrata)
has similar leaves

Bur Oak

(Mossycup Oak)

Quercus macrocarpa

SIZE:
70-80 ft. tall; leaves 6-12 in. long.

WHAT TO LOOK FOR:
leaves large, wedge-shaped, with deep (almost to midrib) indentations near center; acorn cup deep, fringed with stout hairs.

HABITAT:
moist bottomlands (East) to dry grasslands (Midwest).

Birches *Betula*

Thin, often shreddy bark and fine-toothed oval leaves mark the 12 birch representatives (7 trees and 5 shrubs) in North America. Birches are a special delight in winter, when their decorative bark adds color and texture to the snowy landscape. Wintertime birches have another conspicuous feature—dangling clusters of flowers (catkins), which will open and release pollen in spring. After pollination, the female flowers develop into conelike fruits with winged nutlets. Scattered by the wind, the seeds do especially well if they land on mineral soils exposed by fire or deposited by a stream or glacier. Many birches are pioneer trees—species that grow rapidly on bare soil, offer shade to the next wave of invaders (often conifers), and die at an early age. The silvery barked Yellow Birch (*Betula alleghaniensis*) is an exception. It is tolerant of shade and thrives among the beeches and maples of eastern forests.

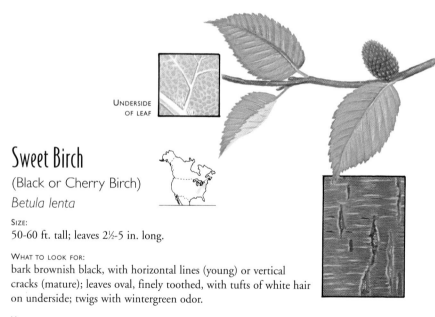

UNDERSIDE OF LEAF

Sweet Birch

(Black or Cherry Birch)

Betula lenta

SIZE:
50-60 ft. tall; leaves 2½-5 in. long.

WHAT TO LOOK FOR:
bark brownish black, with horizontal lines (young) or vertical cracks (mature); leaves oval, finely toothed, with tufts of white hair on underside; twigs with wintergreen odor.

HABITAT:
valleys and slopes in rich, well-drained soil.

Paper Birch
(Canoe Birch)

Betula papyrifera

SIZE:
50-70 ft. tall;
leaves 2-3 in. long.

WHAT TO LOOK FOR:
bark chalky white, peeling in thin strips; leaves coarsely double-toothed; catkins (flowers) yellow-green.

HABITAT:
streambanks, lakeshores, hillsides in moist, sandy soil; often grows in burned-over areas.

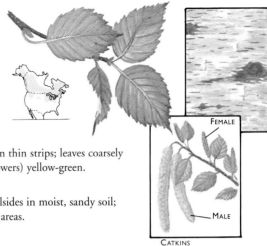

FEMALE

MALE

CATKINS

River Birch
(Red Birch)

Betula nigra

SIZE:
70-80 ft. tall; leaves 1½-3 in. long.

WHAT TO LOOK FOR:
leaves oval, with coarsely double-toothed edges and wedge-shaped base; bark pale red-brown with papery scales and horizontal lines (young) or dark red-brown to gray with thick scales (mature).

HABITAT:
streambanks, wet woods.

Alders *Alnus*

Alders add fertility to soils, for bacteria living on their roots "fix" nitrogen from the air and turn it into nutrients for other plants. Red Alder is the only large tree of the group in North America; others are shrubs or small trees. Alders commonly form tangled thickets along the water's edge.

Red Alder

(Oregon Alder)

Alnus rubra

SIZE:
80-130 ft. tall; leaves 3-6 in. long.

WHAT TO LOOK FOR:
leaves oval, with sunken veins on upper surface, gray-green with reddish hairs on underside; fruits conelike, green (summer) or red-brown (fall); bark gray.

HABITAT:
bottomlands and gentle slopes in moist loam.

Gordonias *Gordonia*

The fragrant flowers of the Loblolly-bay perfume southern verandas during summer. This fast-growing tree is the only North American gordonia—a group belonging to the tea family and named for the British horticulturalist James Gordon.

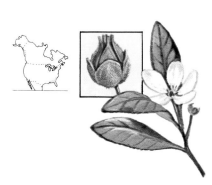

Loblolly-bay

Gordonia lasianthus

SIZE:
40-50 ft. tall; leaves 4-5 in. long.

WHAT TO LOOK FOR:
leaves shiny, evergreen, shallowly toothed; flowers white, with 5 petals; fruits woody, split into 5.

HABITAT:
moist areas.

Hornbeams *Carpinus*

Within the three-dimensional green space of a mature hardwood forest, small shade-tolerant trees thrive beneath the upper canopy. The American Hornbeam is one such understory tree. It reveals its kinship with the birches when catkins develop along with the leaves in spring. Like its relative the Eastern Hop-hornbeam, it is sometimes called Ironwood.

American Hornbeam
(Blue-beech)
Carpinus caroliniana

SIZE:
10-30 ft. tall,
leaves 2-4 in. long.

WHAT TO LOOK FOR:
leaves oval, double-toothed;
fruits triangular, papery, with single nutlet; bark smooth, fluted, blue-gray.

HABITAT: streambanks, bottomlands.

Hop-hornbeams *Ostrya*

Small bladderlike fruits resembling the hops used by brewers characterize the hop-hornbeams. The Eastern Hop-hornbeam, the only widespread North American species in this small group, is also known as Ironwood or Leverwood. Its tough, resilient wood has been used in farm implements.

Eastern Hop-hornbeam
Ostrya virginiana

SIZE:
30-40 ft. tall; leaves 2½-4½ in. long.

WHAT TO LOOK FOR:
leaves oval, double-toothed, with tufts of yellow hair on lower midrib; fruits bladderlike, light brown, in clusters; mature bark in narrow strips curling away from trunk.

HABITAT:
hillsides and ridges with gravelly soils.

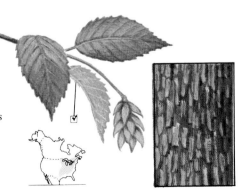

Basswoods *Tilia*

The basswoods, or lindens, supply welcome shade on city streets. Their soft, light-colored wood is a carver's delight. And their pale, fragrant flowers yield nectar that bees transform into a most flavorsome honey. All three North American species have heart-shaped leaves and straplike bracts.

American Basswood

Tilia americana

SIZE:
70-80 ft. tall; leaves 5-6 in. long.

WHAT TO LOOK FOR:
straplike bracts with hanging flowers or nutlets; leaves heart-shaped, coarsely toothed, smooth on both surfaces.

HABITAT:
bottomlands in damp loam.

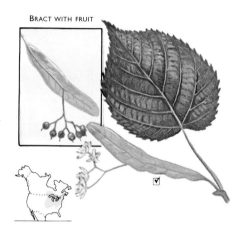

BRACT WITH FRUIT

Cereuses *Cereus*

Highly resistant to drought, the 200-odd species in this group have a thick, rubbery "skin," spongy, water-storing tissues, and moisture-conserving needles instead of leaves. The only common North American tree in the group is the Saguaro.

Saguaro

(Giant Cactus)

Cereus giganteus

SIZE:
50-60 ft. tall; spines 1½ in. long.

WHAT TO LOOK FOR:
leaves spinelike, in clusters; trunk and branches fluted, bright green; flowers white; fruits red.

HABITAT:
desert valleys, slopes, and rocky hills.

Willows *Salix*

Most willows share certain characteristics—lance-shaped leaves, a single caplike scale on the bud, separate male and female catkins (flower clusters), and conspicuous projections at the bases of the leaves. New species, especially shrubby forms in the Arctic, are continually being discovered, and so the worldwide total of three to four hundred is only an estimate. In North America four imports, including the Weeping Willow from Asia, now reproduce in the wild, hybridizing with our native species. Willows never grow far from moist ground. Quick to colonize newly formed sandbars, they help reduce erosion by retaining soil in their fibrous, matted roots. Before the age of plastics, certain low-growing species were commonly harvested for basketmaking—and sometimes still are, in certain parts of the world.

Sandbar Willow

Salix exigua

SIZE:
10-25 ft. tall (often shrubby); leaves 2-7 in. long.

WHAT TO LOOK FOR:
leaves narrowly lance-shaped, with widely spaced teeth; stems gray-green, upright; seed capsules hairy in clusters.

HABITAT:
along watercourses on new sandbars and beaches.

Pussy Willow
(Glaucous Willow)

Salix discolor

SIZE:
10-20 ft. tall; leaves 2-5 in. long.

WHAT TO LOOK FOR:
furry white catkins on twigs in spring; leaves narrow, with widely spaced rounded teeth, dark green above, with whitish bloom below.

HABITAT:
stream margins, swamps, wet meadows.

BUD OF
MALE CATKIN

FEMALE CATKIN

FRUIT

MALE CATKIN

Peachleaf Willow

Salix amygdaloides

SIZE:
30-40 ft. tall; leaves 2½-5 in. long.

WHAT TO LOOK FOR:
leaves broadly lance-shaped, shiny green above, whitish green below, with yellow or orange midrib; twigs orange to red-brown.

HABITAT:
along watercourses; swamps; poorly drained slopes.

Weeping Willow

Salix babylonica

SIZE:
30-40 ft. tall; leaves 3-5 in. long.

WHAT TO LOOK FOR:
long branches and lance-shaped leaves that hang down;
leaves green above, gray-green below; twigs bright yellow.

HABITAT:
planted along watercourses, in wet lawns.

planted range

Black Willow

Salix nigra

SIZE:
50-80 ft. tall; leaves 3-6 in. long.

WHAT TO LOOK FOR:
leaves lance-shaped, with curved tips,
light green below; twigs surrounded
by short, scalelike leaves (stipules).

HABITAT:
along watercourses in wet soils;
swamps.

Poplars *Populus*

Like the closely related willows, poplars are pioneer trees. In northern and mountain forests, they colonize burned-over land and areas of new soil in swathes that turn brilliant gold in fall. The poplars known as cottonwoods prefer streambanks, where they help prevent erosion. All poplar leaves have long stems, but those of the aspens are flattened, making the leaves flutter with the merest breeze. A third group of poplars, known as the balsam poplars, is characterized by sticky, resinous buds that smell like Balsam Fir.

Eastern Cottonwood
Populus deltoides

SIZE:
80-100 ft. tall;
leaves 3-6 in wide.

WHAT TO LOOK FOR:
leaves triangular, with coarse, rounded teeth; leafstalks flattened; end buds sticky (not aromatic); fruit capsules green, with cottony seeds.

HABITAT:
bottomlands.

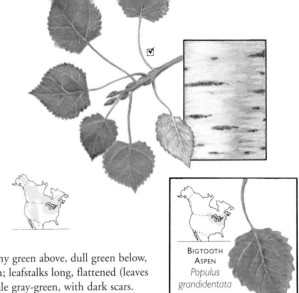

Quaking Aspen

Populus tremuloides

SIZE:
50-60 ft. tall;
leaves 1½-3 in. long.

WHAT TO LOOK FOR:
leaves nearly round, shiny green above, dull green below, with fine, rounded teeth; leafstalks long, flattened (leaves quake in wind); bark pale gray-green, with dark scars.

HABITAT:
variable; in logged or burned-over areas.

BIGTOOTH
ASPEN
Populus grandidentata

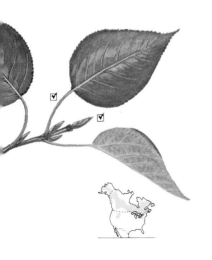

Balsam Poplar

Populus balsamifera

SIZE:
60-80 ft. tall; leaves 3-6 in. long.

WHAT TO LOOK FOR:
leaves oval, sharply pointed, finely toothed, dark green above, rusty to golden brown or whitish below; leafstalks usually round; buds long, pointed, sticky, aromatic.

HABITAT:
bottomlands and along watercourses.

Sourwoods *Oxydendrum*

The name Sourwood derives from the tree's acid-tasting leaves.
Another name, Lily-of-the-valley Tree, refers to its bell-shaped blossoms.
The Sourwood belongs to the heath family, and many other heaths,
including the madrones and blueberries, have flowers of similar form.

Sourwood
(Lily-of-the-valley Tree)
Oxydendrum arboreum

SIZE:
30-50 ft. tall; leaves 5-7 in. long.

WHAT TO LOOK FOR:
leaves elliptical, with small incurved teeth;
flowers bell-like, white; fruit capsules dry, tan.

HABITAT:
dry, gravelly slopes and ridges.

Sweetleaves *Symplocos*

Most of the 350 species of sweetleaves are native to Asia and Australia. Several other groups—for example, beeches and sassafrases—occur mainly in Asia and are represented in the Americas by only one or two species. This distribution has led scientists to speculate that the plants within such a group share an ancestor that existed when, as geologists believe, the continents were united.

Sweetleaf
(Horse-sugar)
Symplocos tinctoria

SIZE:
15-20 ft. tall; leaves 5-6 in. long.

WHAT TO LOOK FOR:
leaves semi-evergreen, elliptical, dark green above, pale green and hairy below; flowers yellow, close to twig; fruits red-brown; bark gray, with warts and fissures.

HABITAT:
deciduous forests in rich, moist soils; edges of swamps; grows as understory tree or shrub.

FRUIT

Persimmons *Diospyros*

Common Persimmon colonizes old fields, its seeds spread by raccoons and opossums feeding on the fruit. Until frost colors it purple-orange, the fruit is paler in color; the equally delectable fruit of Texas Persimmon (*Diospyros texana*) is black. Both trees have fine-grained, ebony-black heartwood.

Common Persimmon
Diospyros virginiana

SIZE:
30-50 ft. tall; leaves 2½-6 in. long.

WHAT TO LOOK FOR:
leaves oval, shiny dark green above, pale green and hairy below; flowers green-yellow; fruits fleshy.

HABITAT:
bottomlands, old fields, hedgerows.

Madrones *Arbutus*

Reddish fruits and loosely curling dark red bark make the three North American madrones, all native to the West, rather easy to identify. Adapted to hot, dry summers, they are usually small and crooked, but the Pacific Madrone grows tall and straight in sheltered areas near sea level.

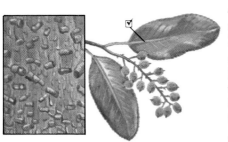

Pacific Madrone
Arbutus menziesii

SIZE:
70-100 ft. tall; leaves 3-5 in. long.

WHAT TO LOOK FOR:
leaves oval, leathery, semi-evergreen, with conspicuous midrib; bark red-brown, curling on branches and young trunks; fruits berrylike, orange-red.

HABITAT:
sea level to slopes in well-drained soils.

Apples *Malus*

Native to Europe and western Asia, the familiar orchard Apple (*Malus sylvestris*) seeds itself readily on this continent and hybridizes with our four native species, all of which are crab apples. Once planted for their tart fruit (an ingredient in jellies and cider), crab apples now serve primarily as ornamental trees.

FRUIT

Oregon Crab Apple
Malus fusca

SIZE:
25-35 ft. tall; leaves 1-4 in. long.

WHAT TO LOOK FOR:
leaves elliptical, sharply toothed, dark green above, pale green below; flowers white, fragrant; fruits oval, yellow tinged with red.

HABITAT:
bottomlands.

FRUIT

Sweet Crab Apple
Malus coronaria

SIZE:
25-30 ft. tall; leaves 2-3 in. long.

WHAT TO LOOK FOR:
leaves oval, with coarse teeth, dark green above, pale green below; thornlike twigs; flowers pink to white, fragrant; fruits yellow-green.

HABITAT:
old fields, edges of woods.

Cherries and Plums *Prunus*

With glorious spring blossoms, fruits favored by animals and humans alike, and wood exceptionally well-suited for cabinetmaking, this group is one of the more valuable members of the rose family. (Apples belong to the rose family too.) Certain species, such as Chokecherry, the most widespread of the 18 native species, form large thickets, benefiting the land by stabilizing the soil. Black Cherry has a poor reputation with dairy farmers. When its leaves fall off in autumn, a normally harmless substance in them decomposes into glucose and cyanic acid. The latter is highly toxic, and poisons cattle that eat the leaves.

American Plum
Prunus americana

SIZE:
20-30 ft. tall; leaves 3-4 in. long.

WHAT TO LOOK FOR:
leaves oval, thick, leathery, with fine double teeth; flowers malodorous; fruits with bright red skin, yellow flesh; trunk distorted, many-branched.

HABITAT:
edges of streams, swamps, and fields in East; dry uplands and mountain slopes in West.

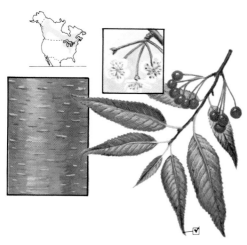

Pin Cherry
(Fire Cherry)
Prunus pensylvanica

SIZE:
10-30 ft. tall (often shrubby); leaves 3-4½ in. long.

WHAT TO LOOK FOR:
leaves lance-shaped, curved inward toward apex, finely toothed; bark thin, with fissures; flowers in clusters of 5-7; fruits bright red.

HABITAT:
variable; often in burned-over areas.

Chokecherry
Prunus virginiana

SIZE:
20-25 ft. tall (usually shrubby); leaves 2-4 in. long.

WHAT TO LOOK FOR:
leaves elliptical (widest above midpoint), finely toothed, hairless below; fruits dark purple-red.

HABITAT:
rich woods, hedgerows, roadsides, riverbanks.

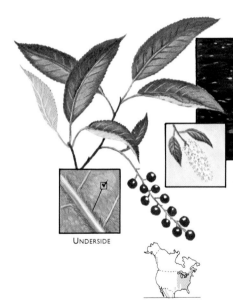

UNDERSIDE

Black Cherry
Prunus serotina

SIZE:
50-60 ft. tall; leaves 2-6 in. long.

WHAT TO LOOK FOR:
leaves elliptical, with long tapered tip, rounded teeth, and rusty hairs along midrib on underside; flowers in long clusters; fruits black when ripe; mature bark peeling, with vertical splits.

HABITAT:
old fields; moist sites in woods.

Mountain-ashes *Sorbus*

The tree most people know by this name is the European species (*Sorbus aucuparia*), sometimes called the Rowan-tree. Widely planted in North America, it reproduces without human help in northern parts of the continent. The orange-red fruits of both the European and the larger-leaved American Mountain-ash are prized by such birds as thrushes, waxwings, and grosbeaks.

American Mountain-ash

Sorbus americana

SIZE:
20-30 ft. tall; leaves 6-8 in. long.

WHAT TO LOOK FOR:
leaves compound, with 13-17 lance-shaped, sharp-toothed leaflets; flowers white, in broad clusters; fruits fleshy, orange-red.

HABITAT:
swamp borders to mountainsides.

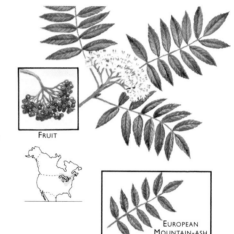

FRUIT

EUROPEAN MOUNTAIN-ASH

Eucalyptuses *Eucalyptus*

The eucalyptuses are native to Australia, but several kinds have been introduced successfully into southern Florida and coastal California. At least one species, the Bluegum, now grows in the wild in California.

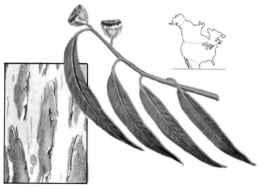

Bluegum Eucalyptus

Eucalyptus globulus

SIZE:
80-120 ft. tall; leaves 4-7 in. long.

WHAT TO LOOK FOR:
leaves evergreen, lance-shaped, curved, gray-green, leathery, aromatic when crushed; bark peeling in long strips; fruit capsules woody, cone-shaped.

HABITAT:
streets, parks, tree farms.

Serviceberries (Shadbushes) *Amelanchier*

Found throughout the continent but scarcely noticeable most of the year, the delicately flowered serviceberries are harbingers of spring, blooming about the same time that shad swim upriver. The fruits, miniature apples with tiny seeds and sweet flesh, disappear rapidly in midsummer, eaten by raccoons, chipmunks, squirrels, and songbirds.

Downy Serviceberry

Amelanchier arborea

SIZE:
30-40 ft. tall; leaves 2-4 in. long.

WHAT TO LOOK FOR:
leaves elliptical, coarsely toothed, hairy when young; flowers white, in drooping clusters (very early spring); fruits berrylike, red to dark purple.

HABITAT:
hillsides, ravines, edges of streams and moist woods.

Hawthorns *Crataegus*

Their seeds spread by birds and deer, the hawthorns colonize abandoned fields. Their thorny, zigzagging branches form impenetrable barriers that protect newly rooted seedlings of other species, which eventually overtop and replace the small, bright-fruited hawthorns. The 35 North American species hybridize readily and are difficult to tell apart.

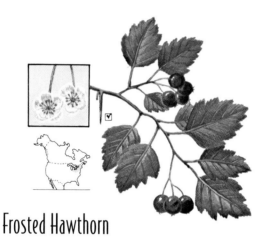

Frosted Hawthorn
Crataegus pruinosa

SIZE:
15-20 ft. tall (often shrubby); leaves 1-2 in. long.

WHAT TO LOOK FOR:
leaves dark blue-green, with 6-8 finely toothed lobes; stout thorns; flowers white; fruits green, ripening to purplish with waxy coat.

HABITAT:
old fields, rocky woods.

Cercocarpus (Mountain-mahoganies) *Cercocarpus*

Members of the rose family, these trees and shrubs of dry mountain slopes of the West are unrelated to true mahoganies. The leaves of the Curlleaf Cercocarpus (*Cercocarpus ledifolius*) curl at the edges and have a white or rusty wool below.

Birchleaf Cercocarpus

Cercocarpus betuloides

SIZE:
10-25 ft. tall; leaves 1-1¼ in. long.

WHAT TO LOOK FOR:
leaves evergreen, margin ⅔-toothed, dark green above, pale green and hairy below, with sunken veins; flowers yellow, with 5 sepals; seed capsules with feathery tail.

HABITAT:
dry open slopes, hillsides.

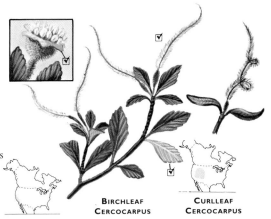

BIRCHLEAF CERCOCARPUS

CURLLEAF CERCOCARPUS

Redbuds *Cercis*

According to legend, the betrayer of Jesus Christ hanged himself from a branch of a Eurasian redbud, hence the alternative name Judas-tree. California Redbud (*Cercis occidentalis*) is the only native species besides Eastern Redbud.

Eastern Redbud

Cercis canadensis

SIZE:
10-20 ft. tall; leaves 3-4½ in. wide.

WHAT TO LOOK FOR:
leaves heart-shaped, thick, leathery; flowers in clusters of 4-8, pink, developing before leaves; pods dark brown, with brown seeds.

HABITAT:
stream borders, mountain slopes.

Coffeetrees

Gymnocladus

Typical members of the legume family (which includes all the trees on pages 86-90), coffeetrees have pealike fruits, compound leaves, and nitrogen-fixing bacteria on the roots. Their hard seeds have a flavor reminiscent of coffee. Only one species is North American; three others occur in Asia.

Kentucky Coffeetree

Gymnocladus dioicus

SIZE:
40-60 ft. tall;
leaves 1-3 ft. long.

WHAT TO LOOK FOR:
leaves doubly compound, with pair of single leaflets at base of stem; pods thick, leathery, with seeds resembling coffee beans.

HABITAT:
bottomlands, ravines, in rich soils.

Mesquites *Prosopis*

Once forming only isolated groves, mesquite now grows in vast thickets, its spread aided by deer, livestock, and other animals feeding on the sweet pods and dispersing the seeds. Overgrazing and fire prevention have also helped the spread of this southwestern plant.

Honey Mesquite
Prosopis glandulosa

SIZE:
5-30 ft. tall; leaves 8-10 in. long.

WHAT TO LOOK FOR:
leaves compound, with leaflets in opposite pairs; pods fat, constricted between seeds; trunk branching from base.

HABITAT:
arid to semi-arid flatlands and foothills.

Locusts *Robinia*

The Black Locust was taken to Europe about 1600, one of the first North American trees to be introduced into the Old World. Its decay-resistant wood makes excellent fence posts, railroad ties, and grapevine stakes. In late spring, clusters of its white blossoms, resembling sweet peas, perfume the air.

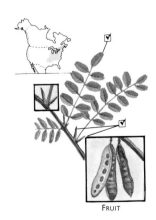

FRUIT

Black Locust
Robinia pseudoacacia

SIZE: 40-60 ft. tall; leaves 8-14 in. long.

WHAT TO LOOK FOR: leaves compound, with oval leaflets notched at apex; pair of spines at leaf base; pods brown, flat, with orange-red seeds.

HABITAT: variable; in rich, moist or limestone soils; planted in hedgerows.

Trees 87

Daleas *Dalea*

The Smokethorn's sparse foliage appears with the spring rains and remains on the tree only a few weeks. When the leaves fall, the tree takes on a smoky look, because of its velvety gray bark. The Smokethorn, the only tree form among the daleas, is one of the few legumes with simple rather than compound leaves.

Smokethorn

(Smoketree, Indigobush) *Dalea spinosa*

FRUIT

SIZE: 15-20 ft. tall; leaves ¾-1 in. long.

WHAT TO LOOK FOR: leaves sparse or absent; sharp spines; bark pale gray, velvety when young; flowers blue; pod with single brown bean.

HABITAT: desert washes.

Acacias *Acacia*

Their name possibly influenced by the Greek word for "thorn," the acacias number about 800 species. Most are native to Africa and Asia, where they are an important source of firewood. The species native to North America occur in the Southwest, where they often form impenetrable thickets.

Gregg Catclaw

(Catclaw Acacia)
Acacia greggii

SIZE: 10-30 ft. tall; leaves 1-3 in. long.

WHAT TO LOOK FOR: leaves doubly compound, with hairy leaflets; spines stout, curved; trunk distorted, with low branches; flowers yellow, fragrant; pods narrow, twisted.

HABITAT: canyons, mesas, mountain slopes.

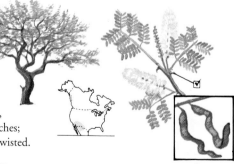

FRUIT

Paloverdes *Cercidium*

Green bark that can photosynthesize compensates for the early loss of leaves on these sometimes shrubby trees. Blue Paloverde (*Cercidium floridum*), which often hybridizes with the Yellow, has blue-green leaflets and flattened, unconstricted pods.

Yellow Paloverde

Cercidium microphyllum

SIZE:
10-15 ft. tall; leaves 2-4 in. long.

WHAT TO LOOK FOR:
leaves compound, appearing after rain; branchlets ending in thorns; bark smooth, yellow-green; flowers brilliant yellow, profuse; pods fat, constricted between seeds.

HABITAT:
desert foothills and plateaus.

Coralbeans *Erythrina*

This is primarily a tropical group, and the Southeastern Coralbean becomes a shrub or an herb north of Florida. The other North American representative, the Southwestern Coralbean (*Erythrina flabelliformis*), is an inhabitant of canyons in southern Arizona and New Mexico. Its red seeds, sometimes used in jewelry, are poisonous, as are all coralbean seeds.

Southeastern Coralbean

Erythrina herbacea

SIZE: 15-20 ft. tall; leaves 6-8 in. long.

WHAT TO LOOK FOR: leaves compound, semi-evergreen, with 3 diamond-shaped leaflets; spines short, curved; flower spikes scarlet, showy; pods with red seeds.

HABITAT: coastal areas in sand.

FRUIT

Honeylocusts *Gleditsia*

In the wild the two North American honeylocusts are easily recognized by the clusters of branching thorns on their trunks. (Some cultivated varieties are thornless.) The Waterlocust (*Gleditsia aquatica*) of southern swamps has smaller leaves and short, oval pods with one to three brown seeds.

Honeylocust

Gleditsia triacanthos

SIZE: 70-80 ft. tall; leaves 5-9 in. long.

WHAT TO LOOK FOR: leaves compound or doubly compound, with elliptical, round-tipped leaflets; twigs with 3-branched thorns; bark dark gray-brown, often thorny; pods flat, twisted, with many seeds.

HABITAT: bottomlands in moist soils.

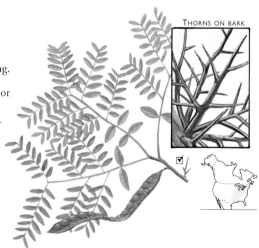

THORNS ON BARK

Mangroves *Rhizophora*

Mangrove fruits germinate on the tree, then drop into the water and take root in the mud. The sturdy, arching prop roots bind the nutrient-rich silt in tidal marshes and build new land. They also act as a nursery for mollusks, crustaceans, young fish, and algae.

Red Mangrove
Rhizophora mangle

SIZE:
15-20 ft. tall; leaves 3½-5 in. long.

WHAT TO LOOK FOR:
trunk branching into aerial roots; leaves evergreen, elliptical, with thick edges; flowers pale yellow, in clusters of 2-3; mature fruits with tubelike tail.

HABITAT:
coastal swamps, estuaries.

White-mangroves *Laguncularia*

The White-mangrove occupies higher ground than the other mangroves; it lives above the high-tide line and along the banks of freshwater streams. After dropping from the tree, the flask-shaped fruits float to new areas and sprout.

White-mangrove
Laguncularia racemosa

SIZE:
20-40 ft. tall; leaves 1½-2½ in. long.

WHAT TO LOOK FOR:
leaves evergreen, oval, leathery, shiny dark green, with red-brown stem; flowers greenish white; fruits oval, berrylike, red-brown; no aerial roots.

HABITAT:
muddy shores of tidal lagoons, bays, and freshwater outflows.

Hollies *Ilex*

Whether evergreen or deciduous, tree-shaped or shrubby, the hollies are most prominent in autumn, when the female plants bear bright red fruits beloved by song and game birds. Eastern North American forests include 14 species, found most often in moist places. Some have marvelous names—Possumhaw, Dahoon (*Ilex cassine*), Yaupon (*Ilex vomitoria*), and Common Winterberry (*Ilex verticillata*).

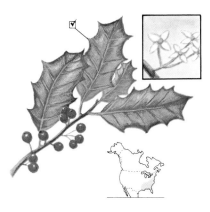

American Holly
Ilex opaca

SIZE:
40-50 ft. tall; leaves 2-4 in. long.

WHAT TO LOOK FOR:
leaves evergreen, stiff, with spiny teeth; fruits berrylike, bright red; flowers greenish white.

HABITAT:
coastal plains in sandy soil; bottomlands with moist, rich soil.

Possumhaw
Ilex decidua

SIZE:
20-25 ft. tall (often shrubby); leaves 2-3 in. long.

WHAT TO LOOK FOR:
leaves deciduous, wavy-edged, rounded at tip, on short shoots; fruits berrylike, orange-red.

HABITAT:
stream and swamp borders; bottomlands.

Tupelos *Nyssa*

Both the common and scientific names of these eastern trees refer to their swampy habitat: "tupelo" comes from Indian words for "swamp tree," and Nyssa was a water nymph in Greek legend. The Water Tupelo (*Nyssa aquatica*) has purple fruit.

Black Tupelo
(Sourgum, Blackgum)
Nyssa sylvatica

SIZE:
60-80 ft. tall; leaves 2-5 in. long.

WHAT TO LOOK FOR:
leaves oval, dark green, often hairy below; bark gray, blocky; fruits deep blue, berrylike.

HABITAT:
bottomlands, slopes.

Buckthorns *Rhamnus*

The 100-plus globally dispersed buckthorns include a number of trees and shrubs with ornamental or medicinal value; the bark of the western Cascara Buckthorn (*Rhamnus purshiana*), for example, is used to make a mild laxative. Thorny branch tips replace the terminal buds on some species, including the European Buckthorn (*Rhamnus cathartica*), which has escaped from cultivation in North America.

Carolina Buckthorn
Rhamnus caroliniana

SIZE:
20-30 ft. tall; leaves 2-6 in. long.

WHAT TO LOOK FOR:
leaves elliptical, sparsely toothed, shiny dark green above, paler and often hairy below; fruits berrylike, black; form may be shrubby.

HABITAT:
streambanks, rich bottomlands, limestone ridges.

Dogwoods *Cornus*

The 15 species of North American dogwoods range from medium-sized trees to small wildflowers. Most are large shrubs. The petals of two trees, Flowering Dogwood and Pacific Dogwood (*Cornus nuttallii*), are actually modified leaves, with the true flowers, greenish yellow in color, clustered in the center.

Flowering Dogwood
Cornus florida

SIZE:
20-30 ft. tall; leaves 3-5 in. long.

WHAT TO LOOK FOR:
leaves oval, with veins curving toward pointed tip; flowers with 4 showy white petallike bracts; fruits red, berrylike, in clusters.

HABITAT:
deciduous forests in well-drained soils.

Soapberries *Sapindus*

In warm water the fruits of this mainly tropical group of 12 species produce a soapy lather; the smooth bony seed inside is poisonous. One of the two North American species is the Wingleaf Soapberry (*Sapindus saponaria*), native to Florida but widely planted elsewhere.

Western Soapberry
Sapindus drummondii

SIZE:
30-40 ft tall; leaves 6-7 in. long.

WHAT TO LOOK FOR:
leaves compound, with 8-18 lance-shaped leaflets (hairy below); fruits yellow, turning black; bark scaly, red-brown.

HABITAT:
canyons, streambanks, dry limestone outcrops.

Buckeyes *Aesculus*

The most widely known buckeye in North America is the Eurasian Horsechestnut, Its six native relatives share certain characteristics: palmately compound leaves (the leaflets radiating from the end of the stem), showy pyramidal flower clusters, and large, green-husked fruit. The Yellow Buckeye (*Aesculus octandra*) of the Appalachian Mountains has smooth fruit.

Ohio Buckeye
(Stinking Buckeye)
Aesculus glabra

SIZE:
40-60 ft. tall; leaves 7-9 in. wide.

WHAT TO LOOK FOR:
leaves palmately compound, with 5 elliptical leaflets; flowers yellow, malodorous, in spikes; fruits with spiny husk and shiny round nut.

HABITAT:
streambanks, bottomlands.

Horsechestnut
Aesculus hippocastanum

SIZE:
40-60 ft. tall;
leaves 8-10 in. wide.

WHAT TO LOOK FOR:
leaves palmately compound, with 7-9 wedge-shaped leaflets; flowers white, in showy spikes; fruits with thorny husk and 2-3 shiny brown nuts.

HABITAT:
streets, parks.

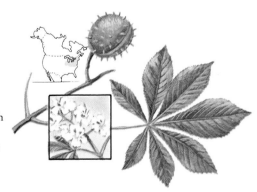

Maples *Acer*

With lobed leaves growing in pairs, most maples are easy to distinguish from other trees. (A few maples, such as the Boxelder, have compound leaves.) Maples also have distinctive fruits called samaras—winged, paired seeds that spin to the earth like tiny helicopters. Some species bear the samaras in spring, others in fall. All produce large quantities of sweet sap in late winter and early spring, but only the Sugar Maple's sap contains enough sugar to warrant commercial tapping and boiling for sugar. Transplanted maple species abound in North America. Pollution-resistant Norway Maples shade city streets and parks, and Oriental species lend a decorative element to many a garden.

Norway Maple
Acer platanoides

SIZE:
60-80 ft. tall;
leaves 4-6 in. wide.

WHAT TO LOOK FOR:
leaves with 5-7 lobes, dark green above, bright green below; crushed stem exudes milky sap; 2 joined seeds with wings spread wide (autumn).

HABITAT:
streets, lawns.

Sugar Maple
Acer saccharum

SIZE:
60-80 ft. tall; leaves 3-5 in. wide.

WHAT TO LOOK FOR:
leaves 5-lobed, bright green above, paler below; 2 joined seeds with nearly parallel wings (autumn); bark gray, with furrows, flakes, or both.

HABITAT:
moist, rich soils in uplands and valleys.

Red Maple
(Swamp Maple)
Acer rubrum

SIZE:
50-70 ft. tall; leaves 2-6 in. wide.

WHAT TO LOOK FOR:
leaves with 3-5 lobes, coarsely toothed, light green above, gray-green below; flowers red, preceding leaves; 2 joined seeds, often red, with wings in narrow V (spring).

HABITAT:
swamps; bottomlands and uplands in moist soils.

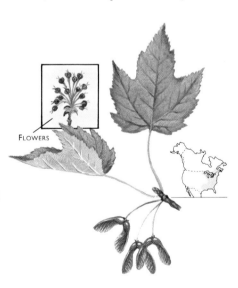

FLOWERS

Silver Maple

Acer saccharinum

SIZE:
60-80 ft. tall; leaves 6-7 in. wide.

WHAT TO LOOK FOR:
leaves 5-lobed, deeply indented, coarsely toothed, pale green above, silvery below; 2 joined seeds with wings at right angles (spring); trunk short, divided into several vertical limbs; crown wide.

HABITAT:
bottomlands in moist soils.

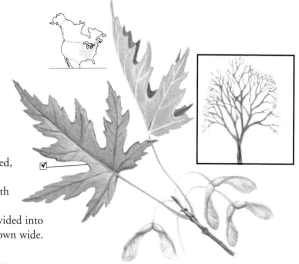

Vine Maple

Acer circinatum

SIZE:
10-20 ft. tall (often shrubby or vinelike); leaves 2-6 in. wide.

WHAT TO LOOK FOR:
leaves with 7-9 lobes, doubly toothed, with prominent veins; flowers deep red; seeds red, with wings spread very wide.

HABITAT:
streambanks; forest openings; beneath conifers.

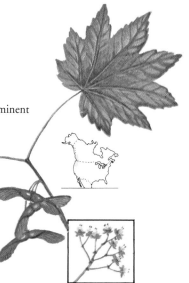

FLOWERS

Rocky Mountain Maple

(Dwarf Maple)

Acer glabrum

SIZE:
20-30 ft. tall;
leaves 5-7 in. long.

WHAT TO LOOK FOR:
leaves 3-lobed (sometimes 5), double-toothed,
often deeply cut, with bright red stalks; seeds green to pink-red.

HABITAT:
along mountain streams; rock ledges, cliffs.

Autumn leaves.

Leaves arc green because they
have chlorophyll, the substance
that enables them to manufacture
food. Other pigments—red,
orange, yellow—are also present
but are masked by the green. As
the days shorten in fall, chlorophyll
synthesis ceases, the green color disappears, and
other pigments begin to dominate. The leaves
of certain species typically turn a uniform color
(yellow on aspens and birches, scarlet on the Red
Maple); others are more variable.

Boxelder

(Ashleaf Maple)

Acer negundo

SIZE:
30-40 ft. tall; leaves 6-15 in. long.

WHAT TO LOOK FOR:
leaves compound, with 3-7 irregularly lobed, coarse-toothed leaflets; flowers yellow-green; seeds elongated, with wings in narrow V (autumn).

HABITAT:
along watercourses; swamp edges.

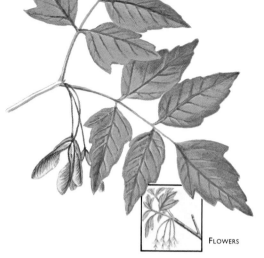

FLOWERS

Striped Maple

(Moosewood)

Acer pensylvanicum

SIZE:
20-30 ft. tall; leaves 5-6 in. long.

WHAT TO LOOK FOR:
leaves 3-lobed, finely toothed, pale below; young bark smooth, bright green with white stripes; flowers bright yellow, on long drooping stalk.

HABITAT:
wooded valleys and slopes in moist soils.

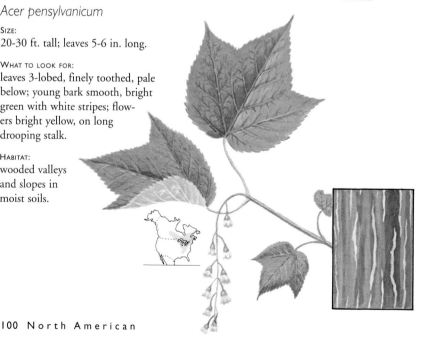

Bigleaf Maple

(Oregon Maple)

Acer macrophyllum

SIZE:
40-50 ft. tall; leaves 8-12 in. wide.

WHAT TO LOOK FOR:
leaves with 5 round, deeply cut
lobes; flowers yellow; seeds hairy,
with wings in V (autumn).

HABITAT:
bottomlands to rocky slopes in
moist soils.

FLOWERS

Sumacs *Rhus*

Although these small trees and shrubs belong to the same family as Poison Sumac and poison ivy, they are not poisonous. In fact, the fruits of Staghorn Sumac and Lemonade Sumac (*Rhus integrifolia*), a California shrub, can be brewed into a lemony tea.

Staghorn Sumac

Rhus typhina

SIZE:
10-20 ft. tall; leaves 16-24 in. long.

WHAT TO LOOK FOR:
leaves compound, with narrowly lance-
shaped, sharply toothed leaflets; leafstalk
hairy; twigs covered with velvety hairs; dense
clusters of dark red, hairy seeds.

HABITAT:
old fields, borders of woodlands.

Ailanthus
(Tree-of-heaven)
Ailanthus altissima

SIZE:
40-60 ft. tall; leaves 1-3 ft. long.

WHAT TO LOOK FOR:
leaves compound; leaflets lance-shaped, with large teeth near stem end; clusters of single-winged seeds remain on tree in winter.

HABITAT:
cities and suburbs in poor dry soils.

Ailanthuses *Ailanthus*

The tree that "grows in Brooklyn" was a Tree-of-heaven, hardiest of the seven or so ailanthuses of the Orient and Australia. A rapid grower, even under urban stress, it has been planted in most major cities of the world, and now grows wild in many places.

Hoptrees *Ptelea*

Brewers occasionally used the fruit of the Common Hoptree as a substitute for hops. Another name, Skunkbush, comes from the pungent odor of the twigs and leaves, and a third, Wafer-ash, from the waferlike fruit and the ashlike compound leaves. The California Hoptree (*Ptelea crenulata*) grows in the canyons and foothills of that state.

Common Hoptree
Ptelea trifoliata

SIZE:
10-15 ft. tall; leaves 4-6 in. long.

WHAT TO LOOK FOR:
leaves compound, with 3 oval leaflets; flowers tiny, greenish white; fruits pale green wafers with single dark seed.

HABITAT:
rock-strewn woods, forest edges.

Prickly-ashes *Zanthoxylum*

Related to lemons, limes, and oranges, the prickly-ashes and the hoptrees (preceding page) are among the few nontropical members of the citrus family. Plants in this family have aromatic oil-containing glands in the bark, fruit, and leaves (in the leaves, the glands show as translucent dots). Prickly-ash bark is a component of certain folk medicines. It was once chewed to relieve toothache, and both species shown here are known as toothache trees.

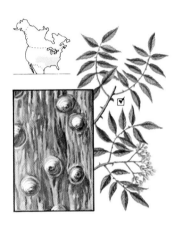

Hercules-club
Zanthoxylum clava-herculis

SIZE:
25-30 ft. tall; leaves 5-8 in. long.

WHAT TO LOOK FOR:
leaves compound, with spiny stalk and toothed leaflets; twigs and (often) bark with stout ½-in.- long spines; flowers green, in clusters.

HABITAT:
riverbanks, bluffs, coastal plains; in sandy soils.

Common Prickly-ash
Zanthoxylum americanum

SIZE:
4-20 ft. tall (often shrubby); leaves 3-5 in. long.

WHAT TO LOOK FOR:
twigs gray, with pair of stout spines at leafstalk joint; leaves compound, with oval leaflets and weak spines on stalks; leaflets and twigs with lemony odor when crushed.

HABITAT:
rock-strewn woodlands, riverbanks.

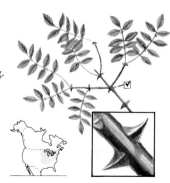

Ashes *Fraxinus*

The typical ash has a compound leaf and a one-seeded fruit with an elongated wing. Only the western Singleleaf Ash (*Fraxinus anomala*) has simple leaves. The White Ash is the most abundant North American species, and the Green Ash (*Fraxinus pennsylvanica*) the most widespread. The Green Ash, which thrives near streams and in moist soil, takes its name from the color of the young twigs.

FRUIT

White Ash

Fraxinus americana

SIZE:
70-80 ft. tall; leaves 8-12 in. long.

WHAT TO LOOK FOR:
leaves compound, with 7 oval, sparsely toothed leaflets; fruits narrow, winged, with seed at stem end; bark with diamond-shaped furrows.

HABITAT:
uplands in rich soils.

Black Ash

Fraxinus nigra

SIZE:
40-50 ft. tall; leaves 12-16 in. long.

WHAT TO LOOK FOR:
leaves compound, with 7-11 lance shaped, finely toothed, stemless leaflets; fruits winged, with flattened seed; bark scaly, with shallow fissures.

HABITAT:
streambanks, floodplains, swamp borders.

Aralias *Aralia*

Devils-walkingsticks sprout rapidly from shallow roots to produce thickets of shoots with just the right appearance for Mephistophelean canes. Other aralias in North America include the shrub Bristly Sarsaparilla (*Aralia hispida*) and two woodland herbs.

Devils-walkingstick

Aralia spinosa

Size: 15-25 ft. tall (sometimes shrubby); leaves 3-4 ft. long.

What to look for: leaves large, doubly compound, with slender prickles on leafstalk; leaflets paired except for 1 at tip and 1 at base of stalk; trunk and branches with many stout spines.

Habitat: woodlands, streambanks.

Black-mangroves *Avicennia*

The name mangrove is used for trees belonging to several groups. The Black-mangrove often grows intermingled with the Red Mangrove or slightly closer to shore. It too helps build and retain shoreline soil.

Black-mangrove

Avicennia germinans

Size: 10-30 ft. tall; leaves 2-3 in. long.

What to look for: leaves evergreen, leathery, with gray fuzz below; fruits pale green, podlike; numerous projecting rootlets at base of tree.

Habitat: tidal shores, swamps.

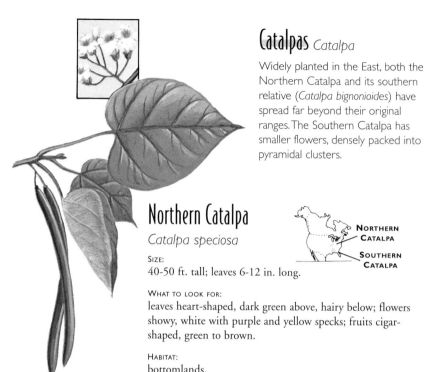

Catalpas *Catalpa*

Widely planted in the East, both the Northern Catalpa and its southern relative (*Catalpa bignonioides*) have spread far beyond their original ranges. The Southern Catalpa has smaller flowers, densely packed into pyramidal clusters.

Northern Catalpa
Catalpa speciosa

NORTHERN CATALPA
SOUTHERN CATALPA

SIZE:
40-50 ft. tall; leaves 6-12 in. long.

WHAT TO LOOK FOR:
leaves heart-shaped, dark green above, hairy below; flowers showy, white with purple and yellow specks; fruits cigar-shaped, green to brown.

HABITAT:
bottomlands.

Fringetrees *Chionanthus*

Common in European gardens, the beautiful, fast-growing Fringetree deserves wider use as a landscape plant in its native land. Fringetrees and ashes belong to the olive family.

Fringetree
(Old-mans-beard) *Chionanthus virginicus*

SIZE:
15-25 ft. tall (sometimes shrubby); leaves 4-8 in. long.

WHAT TO LOOK FOR:
leaves elliptical, with prominent veins; flowers white, fragrant, in feathery clusters of 3; fruits olive-shaped, dark blue, often with waxy bloom.

HABITAT:
streambanks, swamp borders.

Palms *Palmae*

Palm leaves are either featherlike, as on the Florida Royalpalm, or fan-shaped, as on the Cabbage Palmetto and also the Saw-palmetto (in the shrub section). They sprout from a cabbagelike head at the top of the trunk, which is pithy throughout and does not develop annual growth rings. The bark is fibrous.

Unlike all other North American trees except yuccas, palms are monocotyledons: that is, their seedlings have only one leaf (dicotyledons have two). A more conspicuous difference is in the leaf veins. Monocots have parallel veins; dicots are net-veined.

Florida Royalpalm

Roystonea elata

SIZE:
80-100 ft. tall; leaves 12-15 ft. long.

WHAT TO LOOK FOR:
leaves evergreen, compound, dark green; bark gray; upper part of trunk bright green.

HABITAT:
sandy beaches; planted along streets.

Cabbage Palmetto

Sabal palmetto

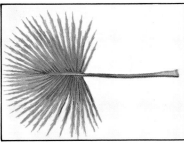

SIZE:
30-50 ft. tall; leaves 7-8 ft. wide.

WHAT TO LOOK FOR:
leaves fan-shaped, sprouting from crown, deeply divided into drooping, bristle-tipped segments; dried leafstalk bases often on upper half of trunk.

HABITAT:
near ocean.

Desert-willows *Chilopsis*

The fragrant blossoms and cigar-shaped fruits of the single species in this group show its close relationship to the catalpas. The long, narrow leaves of this "Desert-catalpa" are better able to resist drought.

Desert-willow

Chilopsis linearis

SIZE:
10-15 ft. tall (often shrubby); leaves 6-12 in. long.

WHAT TO LOOK FOR:
leaves narrow, often sticky when young; flowers showy, white with purple specks; fruits cigar-shaped, dark brown.

HABITAT:
desert depressions, streambanks.

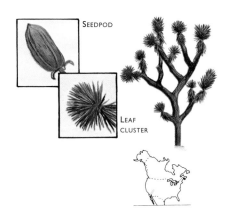

Yuccas *Yucca*

Many people associate yuccas with deserts, but these trees and shrubs of the lily family occur in dry soils elsewhere as well. Because of the sharp, narrow leaves, several species are known as Spanish-bayonet.

SEEDPOD

LEAF CLUSTER

Joshua-tree

Yucca brevifolia

SIZE:
15-40 ft. tall; leaves 6-10 in. long.

WHAT TO LOOK FOR:
leaves evergreen, bayonetlike, sharply toothed, in dense clusters at ends of branches; pods tan, 6 sectioned.

HABITAT:
desert flats and foothills.

Tree and Shrubs.

This is the first of 23 pages on shrubs—woody plants that are usually smaller than trees and have several stems instead of a trunk. Shrubs may occasionally develop into trees, and chances are that a shrub has close relatives that are trees.

Witch-hazels *Hamamelis*

The scraggly Witch-hazel puts forth its curious yellow flowers in fall, after most deciduous plants have lost their leaves. The woody fruit is unusual too; when mature, it ejects its seed a distance of 15 feet or more. The lotion called witch hazel is made from the bark.

FLOWER AND
FRUIT

Witch-hazel

Hamamelis virginiana

SIZE:
5-15 ft. tall; leaves 4-6 in. long.

WHAT TO LOOK FOR:
leaves asymmetrical at base, with coarse rounded teeth; flowers yellow, clustered, with narrow, twisted petals (late fall); fruits hard brown capsules.

HABITAT:
bottomlands, forests, streambanks.

Sweetshrubs *Calycanthus*

With showy flowers and aromatic leaves, the four North American sweetshrubs make attractive landscape plants. The leaf of the Smooth Allspice (*Calycanthus fertilis*) is hairless below.

Carolina Allspice
Calycanthus floridus

SIZE:
3-9 ft. tall; leaves 2-5 in. long.

WHAT TO LOOK FOR:
leaves oval, gray-green, densely hairy below, with camphorlike odor when crushed; flowers red-brown, with strawberry odor; fruits leathery brown capsules.

HABITAT:
streambanks, wooded hillsides in moist soils.

FRUIT

Spicebushes *Lindera*

In bare winter woods spicebush blossoms are a first and welcome sign of spring. The only other North American species in this mainly Asian group is the Hairy Spicebush (*Lindera melissaefolium*) of southern swamps.

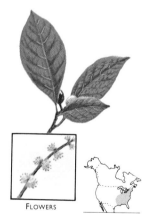

FLOWERS

Spicebush
Lindera benzoin

SIZE:
6-10 ft. tall; leaves 3-4 in. long.

WHAT TO LOOK FOR:
leaves oval, aromatic when crushed; flowers small, close to twig, opening before leaves; berries bright red or yellow.

HABITAT:
swamps, wet woodlands.

Sweet-ferns *Comptonia*

Though its leaves are fernlike, the Sweet-fern is not a fern at all but a flowering plant. Like its relatives the bayberries, it has petalless catkins as flowers; its fruit is a nut with bristly scales.

Sweet-fern

Comptonia peregrina

SIZE:
1-4 ft. tall; leaves 3-5 in. long.

WHAT TO LOOK FOR:
leaves narrow, fernlike, hairy below, fragrant when crushed; twigs brown, hairy.

HABITAT:
fields, logged-over forests.

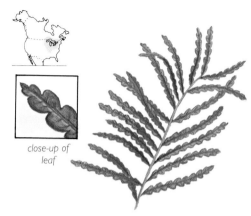

close-up of
leaf

Bayberries *Myrica*

When bayberry fruits are submerged in boiling water, their waxy coating rises to the surface. Candles can be made from the wax of both the Waxmyrtle and the Northern Bayberry (*Myrica pensylvanica*), but do be forewarned: one candle requires several bushels of fruit.

FRUIT

Waxmyrtle

(Southern Bayberry)

Myrica cerifera

SIZE:
10-30 ft. tall; leaves 1½-3 in. long.

WHAT TO LOOK FOR:
leaves lance-shaped, evergreen, dotted with resin; fruits gray, coated with whitish wax.

HABITAT:
swamps; pine and oak woodlands.

Hazels *Corylus*

Lucky is the forager who finds tasty hazelnuts before squirrels and other rodents do.
The nuts called filberts come from Eurasian hazels, not from the two native species.

**AMERICAN
HAZEL**
(*Corylus
americana*)

Beaked Hazel

(Beaked Filbert)

Corylus cornuta

SIZE:
3-9 ft. tall (tree size in California); leaves 2-5 in. long.

WHAT TO LOOK FOR:
leaves oval, sharply toothed, downy below;
twigs hairless; fruits with tubular husks.

HABITAT: old fields, margins of woodland clearings.

Saltbushes *Atriplex*

In dry, nearly barren parts of the West, wild animals and
livestock alike browse on the Four-wing Saltbush and its
spiny relative the Shad-scale (*Atriplex confertifolia*), or
Sheep-fat. Saltbushes do well in seashore gardens.

Four-wing Saltbush

Atriplex canescens

SIZE:
2-4 ft. tall; leaves 1-2 in. long.

WHAT TO LOOK FOR:
leaves narrow, thick, scaly, gray-green; stems whitish;
fruits with pale tan, 4-winged husk.

HABITAT:
salt flats; semideserts to arid foothills.

Cyrillas *Cyrilla*

In Virginia the Swamp Cyrilla's leaves turn orange and scarlet in autumn, but farther south the green leaves persist. The plant occurs not only in the Southeast but also throughout the West Indies and in the swamps of northern South America. One of its names, He-huckleberry, alludes to the belief that Cyrillas are male huckleberry plants.

FLOWERS

Swamp Cyrilla

(Leatherwood)

Cyrilla racemiflora

SIZE:
6-25 ft. tall; leaves 2-4 in. long.

WHAT TO LOOK FOR:
leaves semi-evergreen, elliptical, shiny above with netlike veins below; flowers white to pink; pods yellow; may develop into a tree.

HABITAT:
swamps, streambanks of coastal plains.

Ocotillos *Fouquieria*

Much of the year ocotillos look like thorny dead sticks, but a rain at any time will bring forth the leaves. When the leaves on new growth fall, their sharp-pointed stalks remain to become the thorns.

Ocotillo

Fouquieria splendens

SIZE:
6-20 ft. tall; leaves ½-1 in. long.

WHAT TO LOOK FOR:
branches with stout thorns; fleshy leaves following rain; showy red flowers after winter rain.

HABITAT:
deserts.

Ledums *Ledum*

These low shrubs are typical members of the acid-tolerant heath family. The thick, leathery leaves conserve moisture, and the root system carefully buffers the acidic water entering the plant.

Labrador Tea

Ledum groenlandicum

SIZE:
1-3 ft. tall; leaves 1-2 in. long.

WHAT TO LOOK FOR:
leaves evergreen, narrow, edges rolled under, white or rusty and woolly below; flowers white, 5-petaled.

HABITAT:
bogs, high mountaintops.

Bog Rosemarys *Andromeda*

Usually growing with other heath plants on mountaintops or in cool northern bogs, these plants do well in rock gardens if they have full sun and acid, peaty soil. A number of shrubs sold as "andromeda" belong to other groups.

Bog Rosemary

Andromeda glaucophylla

SIZE: ½-1½ ft. tall; leaves 1-1½ in. long.

WHAT TO LOOK FOR: leaves evergreen, very narrow, with edges rolled under, white below; flowers urn-shaped, white to pink; fruits brown capsules.

HABITAT: bogs; acid, peaty to sandy soils.

Rhododendrons *Rhododendron*

Asia claims a major share of the 800-odd rhododendron species; only 20 shrubs and 3 small trees are North American natives. Some are evergreen, conserving moisture and warmth in winter by rolling their leaves as temperatures drop. (The lower the temperature, the tighter the leaf roll.) The Flame Azalea (*Rhododendron calendulaceum*), which brightens southeastern woodlands with orange flowers in May, is a deciduous species.

Rosebay Rhododendron

(Great Laurel)

Rhododendron maximum

SIZE: 10-20 ft. tall; leaves 4-12 in. long.

WHAT TO LOOK FOR: leaves evergreen, oval, thick, leathery, dark green; flowers white to pink, in large, dense clusters.

HABITAT: moist mountain slopes, streambanks.

Leatherleaves *Chamaedaphne*

In North America, Europe, and Asia, the Leatherleaf, or Cassandra, forms matted tangles that add a bit of a bounce to a bog-walker's step. The plant blooms in early spring.

Leatherleaf

Chamaedaphne calyculata

SIZE:
1-3½ ft. tall; leaves ½-2 in. long.

WHAT TO LOOK FOR:
leaves semi-evergreen, elliptical, leathery, with yellowish scales below; flowers urn-shaped, white, each opposite a small leaf; fruits tan capsules.

HABITAT:
bogs, tundra.

Laurels *Kalmia*

A laurel blossom has 10 pollen-bearing stamens, each tucked into a pouch. When triggered by an insect, the stamens snap toward the center, and pollination occurs. The six native laurels include Lambkill (*Kalmia angustifolia*) and Bog Laurel (*Kalmia polifolia*), both poisonous to livestock if eaten in quantity.

Mountain Laurel

Kalmia latifolia

SIZE:
10-20 ft. tall; leaves 3-4 in. long.

WHAT TO LOOK FOR:
leaves evergreen, elliptical, thick, bunched near branch tip; flowers delicate pink, in showy clusters.

HABITAT:
hills, mountain slopes; in all soils except those with lime.

Manzanitas *Arctostaphylos*

Numbering 50 or more species, the manzanitas occur mainly in warm, dry areas of the American West and in Central America, although the Bearberry (*Arctostaphylos uva-ursi*) lives as far north as the Arctic Circle. Some species are occasionally small trees.

Bigberry Manzanita

Arctostaphylos glauca

SIZE:
6-12 ft. tall; leaves 1-2 in. long.

WHAT TO LOOK FOR:
leaves evergreen, oval, dull green with waxy bloom; fruits berrylike, juicy, with single stone; bark dark red-purple.

HABITAT:
dry mountain slopes.

Chamises *Adenostoma*

Like other resinous plants of the California chaparral, the chamises are highly flammable. "Chamise" comes from the Spanish word for half-burned wood. One species, Redshank (*Adenostoma sparsifolium*), is named for its peeling red bark.

LEAF CLUSTER

Chamise

(Greasewood)

Adenostoma fasciculatum

SIZE:
2-8 ft. tall; leaves ¼-½ in. long.

WHAT TO LOOK FOR:
leaves evergreen, needlelike, leathery, clustered; flowers 5-petaled, white, in dense terminal clusters.

HABITAT:
chaparral, mountain slopes.

Blueberries and Cranberries *Vaccinium*

From Alaska to the Andes and from Norway to the Transvaal, the 300 species of blueberries and cranberries are remarkable for their ability to thrive in a variety of environments. Of the 30 North American species, only the Tree Sparkleberry (*Vaccinium arboreum*) of upland forests in the South gets beyond the shrub stage.

Highbush Blueberry

Vaccinium corymbosum

SIZE:
5-10 ft. tall; leaves 1½-3 in. long.

WHAT TO LOOK FOR:
leaves elliptical, smooth, green; flowers white to pink, urn-shaped; berries blue to blue-black, with slight waxy bloom.

HABITAT:
swamps, moist woodlands, dry uplands.

Lowbush Blueberry

Vaccinium angustifolium

SIZE:
3-15 in. tall; leaves ¼-¾ in. long.

WHAT TO LOOK FOR:
leaves lance-shaped, shiny, bright green, with fine bristle-tipped teeth; flowers white to pink-tinged, urn-shaped; fruits blue-black, with waxy bloom.

HABITAT:
bogs, tundra, dry sandy flats, rocky slopes.

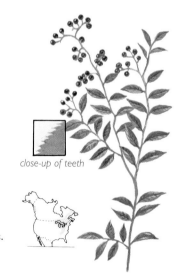

close-up of teeth

Silverbells *Halesia*

The bells of a silverbell are delicate white flowers that dangle from the twigs in spring. Carolina Silverbell grows mainly in the mountains; the other two native species grow on the southeastern coastal plain.

Carolina Silverbell
Halesia carolina

SIZE:
10-30 ft. tall; leaves 3-4 in. long.

WHAT TO LOOK FOR:
leaves elliptical, toothed, somewhat hairy below; flowers white, with shallow lobes; fruits woody, 4-winged; can be shrub or small tree.

HABITAT:
streambanks, slopes.

Snowbells *Styrax*

Snowbells have wider-flaring flowers and rounder fruits than the closely related silverbells. The bark of some Asian species is the source of benzoin, a resin used in medicines and perfumes.

Bigleaf Snowbell
Styrax grandifolius

SIZE:
3-12 ft. tall; leaves 2½-5 in. long.

WHAT TO LOOK FOR:
leaves elliptical to oval, with white hairs below; flowers bell-shaped, white; fruits with pointed tips.

HABITAT:
swamp and stream edges, wet woods.

Brambles *Rubus*

Blackberries, raspberries, dewberries—these delectable fruits all come from closely related species in the rose family. Their leaves are usually compound, and their thorny branches, called canes, often arch toward the ground. A cane leafs out during its first year; the second year it flowers, fruits, and dies. Bramble patches furnish food and shelter for wildlife and protection for seedlings of trees and other shrubs.

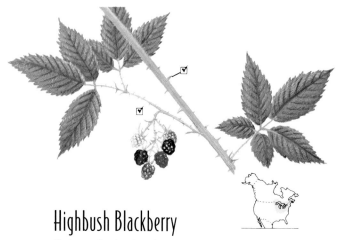

Highbush Blackberry

Rubus allegheniensis

SIZE:
3-7 ft. tall; leaves 3-5 in. long.

WHAT TO LOOK FOR:
leaves compound, with 3 or 5 doubly toothed leaflets, hairy below; leafstalks spiny; fruits black when ripe; canes red-green, with straight thorns.

HABITAT:
old fields, roadsides.

Currants and Gooseberries *Ribes*

Generally, currant branches lack prickles, and the flowers and fruits grow in elongated clusters. In contrast, most gooseberries are prickly, with flowers and fruits in short clusters of one to five. Both groups have maple-shaped leaves.

American Black Currant

Ribes americanum

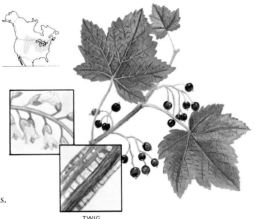

SIZE:
2-4 ft. tall; leaves 1-3 in. long.

WHAT TO LOOK FOR:
leaves with 3 large and 2 small lobes, coarsely toothed, dotted with resin on both sides; leafstalks bristly; flowers yellow-white; fruits shiny, red-black; twigs ridged.

HABITAT:
bottomlands, slopes, openings in woods.

TWIG

Toyons *Heteromeles*

The Toyon, like other plants of the chaparral and adjacent woodlands, sprouts readily after fire or cutting. Often planted as an ornamental, the fruiting Toyon offers a vivid display of red and green, certain to call holly to mind. Birds eat its small "apples."

Toyon

(Christmas-berry)

Heteromeles arbutifolia

SIZE: 6-12 ft. tall; leaves 2-4 in. long.

WHAT TO LOOK FOR: leaves evergreen, elliptical, leathery, sharply toothed; flowers 5-petaled, white, in terminal sprays; fruits red.

HABITAT: foothills, canyons, chaparral.

Roses *Rosa*

So familiar is the rose that hardly any explanation is needed beyond Gertrude Stein's "Rose is a rose is a rose is a rose." But botanists have so transformed roses that one tends to forget that wild ones have only five simple petals, most often pink. Among the other distinguishing traits are the arching or climbing form, the stipules (winglike structures at the base of the leafstalk), the thorns, and the bright hips (fruits).

Multiflora Rose

Rosa multiflora

Size: 3-6 ft. tall; leaves 3-5 in. long.

What to look for: leaves compound, with 7 oval, toothed leaflets; fringed stipules at leafstalk base; twigs bright green, with stout thorns; flowers 5-petaled, white; fruits red; branches arching.

Habitat: old fields, roadsides.

Prairie Rose

Rosa setigera

Size: 4-6 ft. tall; leaves 2-4 in. long.

What to look for: leaves compound, with 3 (rarely 5) oval, toothed leaflets; twigs with small thorns; flowers 5-petaled, pale to deep pink; fruits red; branches arching or climbing.

Habitat: prairies, woodland thickets.

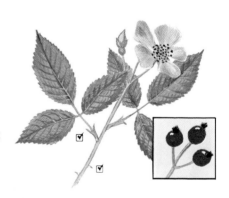

Dogwoods *Cornus*

Tree, shrub, wildflower—this group has representatives in all three categories. Dogwood leaves usually grow in pairs (opposite one another on the twig); an exception is the Alternate-leaf Dogwood. The leaf veins characteristically curve away from the central vein and then bend to follow the edge of the leaf. The small clustered flowers of dogwood shrubs lack the showy petallike bracts of the Flowering Dogwood tree and the bunchberry wildflower.

Red-osier Dogwood
Cornus stolonifera

SIZE: 3-7 ft tall; leaves 2-5 in. long.

WHAT TO LOOK FOR: leaves oval, dark green above, whitish below; flowers white, in rounded clusters; fruits berrylike, white; stems crimson in winter, white inside.

HABITAT: near swamps and bogs; wet sites in forests.

FRUIT

FRUIT

Alternate-leaf Dogwood
Cornus alternifolia

SIZE: 5-10 ft. tall; leaves 3-5 in. long.

WHAT TO LOOK FOR: leaves oval, bright yellow-green above, pale green below, arranged alternately on twig; flowers white, in broad clusters; fruits berrylike, dark blue, with red stems; stems and twigs dark red-brown.

HABITAT: mixed woods in moist, rich soils.

Ceanothuses *Ceanothus*

Although the 60 or so species are concentrated in California (some are known as California-lilacs), ceanothuses have been planted around the world for their beautiful blossoms. One of the few eastern species, the white-flowered New Jersey Tea (*Ceanothus americanus*), was reputedly used as a tea substitute during the Revolutionary War. The roots of New Jersey Tea and some other species yield a red dye and also substances used in the past to congeal blood.

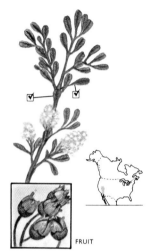

FRUIT

Buckbrush
Ceanothus cuneatus

SIZE:
3-8 ft. tall; leaves ½-1 in. long.

WHAT TO LOOK FOR:
leaves evergreen, narrow at base, dull gray-green above; wartlike bumps at bases of twigs; flowers white, lavender, or blue; fruit capsules with 3 horns.

HABITAT:
dry mountain slopes.

Blueblossom
Ceanothus thyrsiflorus

SIZE:
5-15 ft. tall; leaves ¾-2 in. long.

WHAT TO LOOK FOR:
leaves evergreen, broadly oval, with 3 main veins; flowers blue, in branching clusters; fruits with 3 lobes; may be treelike or a creeping mat.

HABITAT:
dry slopes of foothills and mountains.

FRUIT

Creosote Bushes *Larrea*

Creosote bushes are adapted to desert living. Where they are the dominant plants, they often grow in evenly spaced rows—a "self-imposed" method of rationing water. A strong-smelling resin coats the leaves, reducing moisture loss.

Creosote Bush

Larrea tridentata

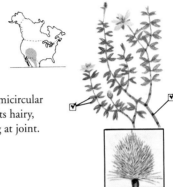

SIZE:
3-9 ft. tall; leaves ⅜ in. long.

WHAT TO LOOK FOR:
leaves evergreen, compound, with 2 semicircular olive-green leaflets; flowers yellow; fruits hairy, white; branches jointed, with dark ring at joint.

HABITAT:
deserts.

FRUIT

Burningbushes *Euonymus*

Though concentrated in eastern Asia, the burningbushes have four North American representatives, including one western species. The typical fruit is a brightly colored capsule with a brightly colored coat (bittersweets have similar fruit). The name, however, derives from the scarlet autumn leaves.

Eastern Burningbush

(Wahoo)

Euonymus atropurpureus

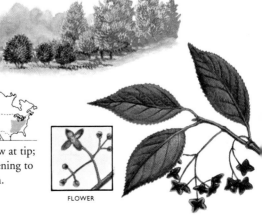

SIZE:
10-15 ft. tall; leaves 2-5 in. long.

WHAT TO LOOK FOR:
leaves elliptical, finely toothed, narrow at tip; flowers purple; fruits bladderlike, opening to reveal red seeds; may be tree in South.

HABITAT:
woodland edges in moist soils.

FLOWER

Bladdernuts *Staphylea*

With inflated fruit capsules containing large bony seeds, the two North American species in this group are easy to identify. The Sierra Bladdernut (*Staphylea bolanderi*) grows in the mountains of California.

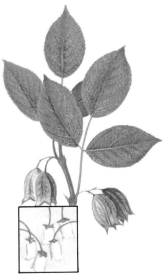

American Bladdernut

Staphylea trifolia

SIZE:
6-12 ft. tall; leaves 6-8 in. long.

WHAT TO LOOK FOR:
leaves compound, with 3 finely toothed leaflets; flowers bell-shaped, in drooping clusters; fruits papery, lantern-shaped, with brown seeds rattling inside.

HABITAT:
forest edges.

Forestieras *Forestiera*

These shrubs and small trees belong to the olive family and have small olivelike fruits; indeed, some species, such as the Florida-privet (*Forestiera segregata*), are even called Wild-olive. The privets used in hedges belong to a different part of the olive family.

Swamp-privet

Forestiera acuminata

SIZE:
3-9 ft. tall (tree form to 30 ft.);
leaves 2-4½ in. long.

WHAT TO LOOK FOR:
leaves elliptical, with pointed apex and base; flowers clustered on twigs, opening before leaves; fruits fleshy, dark purple.

HABITAT:
stream and swamp edges.

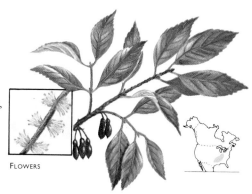

FLOWERS

Poison Sumacs *Toxicodendron*

Sumacs (*Rhus* species) and poison sumacs differ in at least one major detail: only the latter are poisonous (*Toxicodendron* means "poison tree"). Two notorious poison sumacs are poison ivy and poison oak.

Poison Sumac

Toxicodendron vernix

SIZE: 6-10 ft. tall; leaves 7-14 in. long.

WHAT TO LOOK FOR: leaves compound, with 7-13 oval, untoothed leaflets; leafstalks often red; fruits white, hanging in loose clusters (may remain in winter); twigs gray-brown, dotted; may be shrub or tree.

HABITAT: bogs, swamps.

LEAFLESS TWIG

FRUIT

Buttonbushes *Cephalanthus*

Viewed through a magnifying glass, a buttonbush flower cluster shows exquisite detail. Each of the tiny blossoms has petals fused into a narrow tube, a long and wispy pistil, and nectar glands at the base. Bees are a primary pollinator.

Buttonbush

(*Honey-balls*)

Cephalanthus occidentalis

SIZE:
5-15 ft. tall; leaves 2-7 in. long.

WHAT TO LOOK FOR:
leaves oval, shiny, dark green above; flowers fragrant, whitish, in globe-shaped clusters; fruits round, warty, red-brown.

HABITAT: swamps, pond and stream borders.

Elders *Sambucus*

Pithy and easily hollowed out, elder
twigs make excellent whistles and drinking straws.
Though wine is made from the fruits of some species, others, such as the Pacific Red Elder (*Sambucus callicarpa*), have
inedible or even poisonous fruit.

American Elder

(Elderberrry)

Sambucus canadensis

SIZE:
3-10 ft. tall; leaves 4-9 in. long.

WHAT TO LOOK FOR:
leaves compound, usually with 7 elliptical, sharply toothed
leaflets; flowers creamy white, in broad clusters; fruits
berrylike, purple-black; twigs pithy, white inside.

HABITAT: swamp edges; along fences and roads.

Honeysuckles *Lonicera*

Some honeysuckles are shrubs and others vines. One common shrub, the Tatarian
Honeysuckle (*Lonicera tatarica*), is not a native species. An escape from gardens, it grows
wild in the woods, shading out native plants.

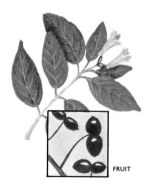

FRUIT

Fly Honeysuckle

Lonicera canadensis

SIZE:
2-4 ft. tall; leaves 1½-3 in. long.

WHAT TO LOOK FOR:
leaves oval, with long fine hair on
margins and stalks; flowers tubular,
yellowish (often red-tinged), in pairs;
berries red, in pairs.

HABITAT:
forests in rich, moist soils.

Viburnums *Viburnum*

Common in shady forests, the viburnums are treasured ornamentals. On many species the leathery, opposite leaves assume brilliant fall colors. The flower clusters are showy and often delightfully scented, and the eye-catching fruits may decorate the shrubs well into winter.

Hobblebush

Viburnum alnifolium

SIZE:
3-9 ft. tall; leaves 4-6 in. long.

WHAT TO LOOK FOR:
leaves broadly oval to heart-shaped, rusty-haired below, with fine irregular teeth; flowers in broad clusters, large at edge of cluster; fruits berrylike, purple-black when ripe; branches horizontal, often rooted at tip.

HABITAT:
cool moist forests.

Nannyberry

Viburnum lentago

SIZE:
10-30 ft. tall; leaves 2-4 in. long.

WHAT TO LOOK FOR:
leaves oval, curved in at tip, sharply toothed; flowers in broad clusters; fruits berrylike, long-stalked, dark blue when ripe, with pointed tips; may be small tree.

HABITAT:
swamp and forest edges.

TWIG
WITH
BUDS

Rabbitbrushes *Chrysothamnus*

Not only rabbits but also deer and other large mammals browse these common desert and high-plain shrubs. The species shown owes the second part of its scientific name to the disagreeable odor of its leaves.

Rabbitbrush

Chrysothamnus nauseosus

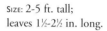

SIZE: 2-5 ft. tall; leaves 1½-2½ in. long.

WHAT TO LOOK FOR: leaves narrow, covered with white hairs; branches matted with hairs; flowers golden yellow, in showy clusters of many heads, each head with 5 florets.

HABITAT: deserts, plains, arid slopes.

HAIRY TWIG AND LEAVES

Sagebrushes *Artemisia*

So abundant are sagebrushes in the arid West that they typify the cold, high desert of the Great Basin. But species in this group occur across the continent. For example, the Dusty-miller (*Artemisia stelleriana*), a perennial herb from Asia with gray, hairy leaves and stems, has colonized eastern beaches.

Common Sagebrush

Artemisia tridentata

SIZE: 2-8 ft. tall; leaves ½-1½ in. long.

WHAT TO LOOK FOR: leaves narrow, 3-toothed at tip, silvery, hairy, aromatic; flowers in terminal clusters; trunk twisted, many-branched.

HABITAT: plains, high deserts.

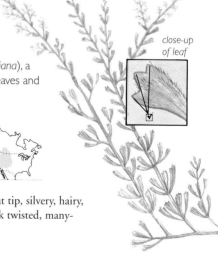

close-up of leaf

Baccharises *Baccharis*

The Groundsel-tree is most conspicuous in autumn, when it blossoms and produces fluffy white fruit similar to a dandelion's. In the West several species with similar flowers and fruit but narrower leaves grow in stream valleys and washes.

FLOWER

FRUIT

Groundsel-tree

Baccharis halimifolia

SIZE: 3-12 ft. tall; leaves 1-3 in. long.

WHAT TO LOOK FOR: leaves diamond-shaped, roughly toothed or shallowly lobed, gray-green, dotted with resin; flowers tiny, in fall; fruit capsules bristling with white hairs.

HABITAT: seashores, tidal marshes, banks of estuaries.

Saw-palmettos *Serenoa*

Saw-palmettos commonly grow in dense thickets beneath pines, their stems creeping along the ground. Rarely does the stem become tall and the plant tree-like. Creamy white flowers bloom amongst the fans, and the small fruit is black and olivelike.

Saw-palmetto

Serenoa repens

SIZE: 3-6 ft. tall; leaves 1-3 ft. wide.

WHAT TO LOOK FOR: leaves fan-shaped, slit more than halfway to base; leafstalks with stout recurved spines; stems often creeping.

HABITAT: pine barrens, hammocks, sand dunes.

NONFLOWERING PLANTS

"**B**ut there's nothing there!" some children complained as they peered into a terrarium alive with ferns, mosses, and other small plants. They were looking, of course, for animal life, and to them all the greenery was background, not substance.

Out in the wild, people often have much the same response. Trees, wildflowers, mammals, and birds are the attention getters, not the humble mosses and ferns. Nonflowering plants have neither size nor coloration to grab your attention. (Except for ferns and close relatives of ferns, the nonflowering plants lack an internal system for transporting water, so they can't grow very high above the ground.) No colorful flowers or fruits add sparkle to their greenish or brownish foliage. (Tiny spores, not flowers and fruits, are their means of reproduction.)

But any feeling of sameness dissolves as you begin to consider these plants as individual entities rather than as backdrops to animal life. In just a single small area you may discover a multitude of species—starlike mosses, strange-looking lichens, ferns with a diversity of texture, color, and form. Just a few feet away, in a spot with different moisture conditions, the species may be completely different. Nor will a particular plant always look the same. For instance, as the year progresses, fiddleheads unfurl into fronds, then spore stalks develop, and finally leaves become burnished by the touch of fall.

Where to Find Nonflowering Plants

The complex life cycles of nonflowering plants cannot be completed without water. But certain species can survive extreme exposure to sun, wind, and drought. For example, drought causes many mosses and lichens (and a few ferns too) to become brown and shriveled, but eventually they will be "resurrected" by rain.

In North America swampy forests have the greatest variety of nonflowering plants and the most luxuriant growth. Royal Ferns extend their arching fronds, and mosses of many types festoon the fallen logs. In other moist areas, different plants predominate. Sphagnum mosses are frequently found in bogs, Bracken fern in fields, quillworts along the shores of quiet lakes and ponds.

Rocky places furnish good hunting, especially where a crevice or overhanging ledge means greater moisture and shade. Even on prairies and plains, where grasses and other hardy flowering plants usually have the upper hand, scattered boulders can create isolated microenvironments in which mosses and lichens come into their own.

Though nonflowering plants tend to hug the ground, sometimes you'll find them by looking up, not down. Representatives of a number of groups—lichens, liverworts, freshwater algae, mosses—live on tree bark (and not just on the north side, as legend would have it); and especially in warm, moist places, ferns may be found out on a limb.

HOW TO USE THE NONFLOWERING PLANTS SECTION

Of all the nonflowering plants, ferns are the most likely to catch your eye, and so ferns receive the most extensive coverage in this section. Generally more massive and obvious than other nonflowering plants, ferns and fern allies (that is, close relatives of ferns) are more complex in organization, as will become evident to you if you look closely at a leaf or a cross section of stem.

• Ferns are shown on pages 136 through 167. Fern allies are on pages 167 through 173. These include clubmosses, spikemosses, quillworts, and horsetails—plants that look very different from ferns but share certain characteristics of structure and reproduction.

• Mosses, liverworts, and hornworts—plants usually less than an inch tall, often growing in a cushion or matt—are shown on pages 174 through 181. Most mosses look like tiny, leafy shoots, with each shoot sometimes bearing a hairlike stalk with a spore case at its tip. (The spore case on the species shown opposite is of a different type, nearly hidden by the leaves.) Important in the identification of mosses, spore cases are also a source of entertainment: if you pinch them open at the appropriate stage of ripeness, a dust cloud of spores wafts away.

• Seaweeds (marine algae) are covered on pages 182 through 191. The species shown on page 135, Dulse, is classified as a red seaweed; the other categories are green and brown.

• On pages 192 through 197 are the lichens, peculiar combinations of algae and fungi living together in relationships that benefit them both. There are three types: the crustose lichens (which form thin crusts), the foliose lichens (these are flat and leaflike), and the fruticose lichens (branching like miniature shrubs). Many lichens, such as the one shown on page 135, are a distinctive grayish or brownish green, their green color modified by the strands of fungus mingling with the algae. British Soldiers, one of the fruticose species, has scarlet tips; certain other species are also red or orange, in part or in their entirety.

• Mushrooms and other fungi, sometimes grouped with the non-flowering plants (they too reproduce by spores), are covered in a separate section beginning on page 198.

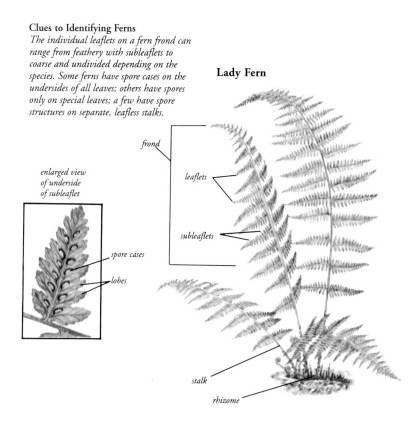

Clues to Identifying Ferns
The individual leaflets on a fern frond can range from feathery with subleaflets to coarse and undivided depending on the species. Some ferns have spore cases on the undersides of all leaves; others have spores only on special leaves; a few have spore structures on separate, leafless stalks.

Lady Fern

frond

enlarged view
of underside
of subleaflet

leaflets

subleaflets

spore cases

lobes

stalk

rhizome

Lichens

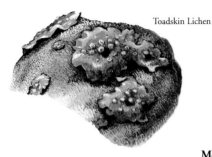

Toadskin Lichen

Mosses

enlarged view
of spore case

Seaweeds

Rock Moss

Dulse

Ferns. Graceful, airy, and delicate in appearance, ferns have a more subtle beauty than wildflowers, and appreciating them—like identifying them—may require a closer look. Though the typical fern is rather lacy, some species are less finely cut; the leafy fronds may be undivided or divided once (into leaflets), twice (into leaflets and subleaflets), or three times (into leaflets, subleaflets, and lobes). Ferns reproduce by spores, which commonly occur on the underside of the frond but in some species are borne on separate stalks. Fronds (or parts of fronds) with spores are called fertile; those without, sterile. A fern's rhizomes—the rootlike stems that creep on or just below the surface—may also be useful in identification. For a detailed discussion of ferns and other nonflowering plants, consult pages 132-135.

STERILE
SUBLEAFLETS

Royal Ferns *Osmundaceae*

These regal ferns are common and conspicuous in eastern wetlands (there are none in the West). The fronds arch out for more than 2 feet; the stalks and roots form large mounds. Plant nurseries use the root masses, popularly known as osmunda, for growing orchids and other plants not requiring soil. Ferns in this family produce spores, in brown or blackish clusters, that die unless they germinate in a week or two.

Royal Fern
Osmunda regalis

SIZE: 2-4 ft. tall.

WHAT TO LOOK FOR: large clumps growing from conspicuous root ball; subleaflets large; spore cases in dense clusters at top of fronds; stalks reddish on shaded individuals.

HABITAT: swamps, marshes.

SPORES: Apr.-June.

Cinnamon Fern

Osmunda cinnamomea

SIZE: 2-3 ft. tall.

WHAT TO LOOK FOR: large clumps of fronds; fertile fronds with masses of spore cases (fronds and cases green, turning brown); leaflets on sterile fronds not cut to vein, with brown woolly tuft below base.

HABITAT: swamps, marshes, wet woods. SPORES: Apr.-June.

Interrupted Fern

Osmunda claytoniana

SIZE: 2-3 ft. tall.

WHAT TO LOOK FOR: fertile fronds interrupted by spore-bearing leaflets (or bare near center); other fronds arching outward; leaflets not cut to vein, slightly longer at center of stalk.

HABITAT: moist woods, roadsides. SPORES: May-June.

Grape Ferns and Adder's Tongues *Ophioglossaceae*

Although these peculiar ferns baffle botanists (their relationship to other ferns is unclear), they are easy to separate from other families; nearly all species in this group have a single stalk with a leafy branch at the side and an upright spore-producing spike. Once thought to be rare, these ferns are often overlooked because they resemble other plants or because they are hidden by other vegetation. Prime sites for finding them include moist grassy areas, fields, open woods, and, in the Southeast, cemeteries.

SUBLEAFLETS

Rattlesnake Fern

Botrychium virginianum

SIZE:
2-18 in. tall.

WHAT TO LOOK FOR:
single stalk with triangular almost horizontal frond divided into lacy leaflets; grapelike clusters of spore cases at top of upright spike.

HABITAT:
rich woods.

SPORES:
May-July.

Adder's Tongue

Ophioglossum vulgatum

SIZE:
6-10 in. tall.

WHAT TO LOOK FOR:
single unfernlike leaf with blunt tip; spore cases in 2 rows at swollen tip of upright spike.

TIP OF FERTILE SPIKE

HABITAT:
woods; meadows; marsh edges; damp grassy ditches.

SPORES:
June-Aug.

Curly Grass Ferns and Climbing Ferns *Schizaeaceae*

These plants look like anything but ferns. Some—the climbing ferns—resemble ivy; others, such as the Curly Grass Fern (*Schizaea pusilla*) of northeastern bogs, look remarkably like grass (a small spore-bearing cluster at the top of the fertile stalk unmasks them as ferns).

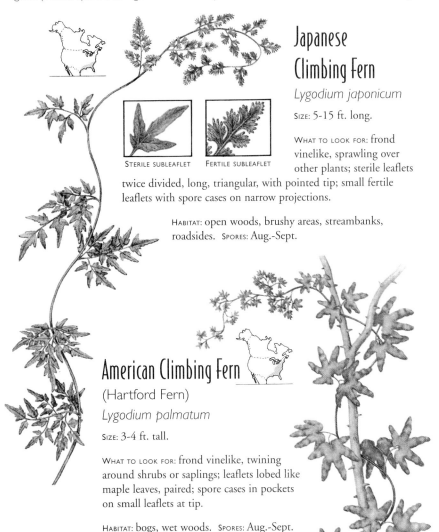

STERILE SUBLEAFLET   FERTILE SUBLEAFLET

Japanese Climbing Fern

Lygodium japonicum

SIZE: 5-15 ft. long.

WHAT TO LOOK FOR: frond vinelike, sprawling over other plants; sterile leaflets twice divided, long, triangular, with pointed tip; small fertile leaflets with spore cases on narrow projections.

HABITAT: open woods, brushy areas, streambanks, roadsides. SPORES: Aug.-Sept.

American Climbing Fern

(Hartford Fern)

Lygodium palmatum

SIZE: 3-4 ft. tall.

WHAT TO LOOK FOR: frond vinelike, twining around shrubs or saplings; leaflets lobed like maple leaves, paired; spore cases in pockets on small leaflets at tip.

HABITAT: bogs, wet woods. SPORES: Aug.-Sept.

Maidenhair Ferns and Relatives *Adiantaceae*

Of all ferns, this group is the most xerophytic—that is, adapted to life in dry places. Although the Northern Maidenhair and several other species live in forests, most grow in rocky places. The Southern Maidenhair (*Adiantum capillusveneris*), for example, flourishes on limestone dampened by waterfall spray—and not just in southern states, but also northward through the Rockies into Canada. This species, along with several close relatives, does well as a house plant, provided it is kept cool.

Maidenhair ferns tend to be small. Although some species, such as the lip ferns, spread out linearly along the underground rootstock, most have clusters (tufts) of fronds. In the clustering species the stalks—often as black, fine, and shiny as a maiden's hair—form small, tight masses.

The spores of these ferns develop not on special stalks but on the leaflets themselves, generally along the veins. In some species the leaf edges roll over the spores, protecting them as they develop. Such rolled-over edges are called false indusia. True indusia (the word *indusium* is Latin for "tunic") are thin protective covers that grow over the spores in the tree fern family and in the spleenworts.

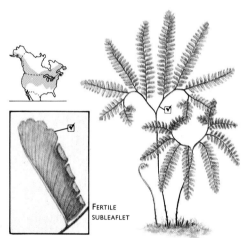

Northern Maidenhair
Adiantum pedatum

Size: 12-24 in. tall.

What to look for: fan-shaped whorls of leaflets held horizontally; subleaflets oblong, toothed on one edge, with spore cases along toothed edge; black, wiry stalks.

FERTILE SUBLEAFLET

Habitat: rich woods.

Spores: Aug.-Oct.

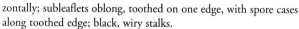

Goldback Fern

Pityrogramma triangularis

SIZE: 5-15 in. tall.

WHAT TO LOOK FOR: fronds triangular, twice divided, green on top, bright yellow to white below; spore cases on underside, scattered along veins.

HABITAT: shaded, damp crevices on rocky slopes and streambanks. SPORES: May-July.

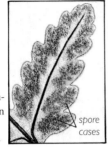

FERTILE SUBLEAFLET

spore cases

Parsley Fern

(American Rock Brake)

Cryptogramma acrostichoides

SIZE: 5-10 in. tall.

WHAT TO LOOK FOR: fronds smooth, leathery, shiny; sterile fronds with short, wide, toothed subleaflets; fertile fronds tall, upright with narrow subleaflets; edge of fertile subleaflet rolled over spore cases.

HABITAT: cliffs, talus slopes.

SPORES: July-Sept.

FERTILE SUBLEAFLET

STERILE SUBLEAFLET

Slender Lip Fern

Cheilanthes feei

SIZE: 4-10 in. tall.

WHAT TO LOOK FOR: very finely divided into tiny round segments; fine white hairs above, dense rusty hairs below; stalks hairy; edge of fertile segment rolled over spore cases.

HABITAT: dry, shaded rock crevices; cliffs. SPORES: July-Sept.

FERTILE SEGMENTS

California Maidenhair

Adiantum jordanii

SIZE: 6-12 in. tall.

WHAT TO LOOK FOR: fronds wide, spreading, not horizontal; subleaflets semicircular with veins in fan shape, on stems; spore cases on rounded edge of subleaflet.

HABITAT: shaded, moist slopes; streambanks. SPORES: June-July.

FERTILE SUBLEAFLET

FERTILE SUBLEAFLET

Lace Fern

Cheilanthes gracillima

SIZE: 4-10 in. tall.

WHAT TO LOOK FOR: stalks in clumps; subleaflets elliptical, smooth and dark green above, densely hairy and white to rusty below; spore cases partly covered by rolled edge of subleaflet.

HABITAT: rock crevices in mountains.

SPORES: July-Sept.

Hairy Lip Fern

Cheilanthes lanosa

SIZE: 10-18 in. tall.

WHAT TO LOOK FOR: stalks scattered (not in clumps); leafy part narrow, longer than lower part of stalk, with rusty hairs (denser below); spore cases partly covered by rolled edge of subleaflet.

HABITAT: rocks, cliffs.

SPORES: July-Sept.

FERTILE SUBLEAFLET

FERTILE LEAFLET

Purple Cliff Brake

Pellaea atropurpurea

SIZE: 10-20 in. tall.

WHAT TO LOOK FOR:
stalks purple-brown to black, slightly hairy; leaflets and subleaflets large and lance-shaped, triangular, or heart-shaped; fertile fronds taller than sterile; spore cases covered by rolled edge of leaflet.

HABITAT: crevices in limestone. SPORES: July-Oct.

Smooth Cliff Brake

Pellaea glabella

SIZE: 5-15 in. tall.

WHAT TO LOOK FOR: similar to but smaller than Purple Cliff Brake, with shinier, redder, hairless stalks; fertile and sterile fronds alike; spore cases covered by rolled edge.

HABITAT: crevices in limestone.

SPORES: July-Sept.

FERTILE SUBLEAFLET

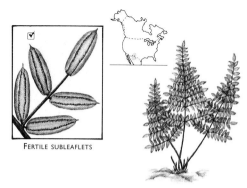

FERTILE SUBLEAFLETS

Spiny Cliff Brake
Pellaea truncata

SIZE: 5-15 in. tall.

WHAT TO LOOK FOR: very stiff fronds; leaflets at right angle to stalk, divided into small boat-shaped subleaflets with sharp tips; spore cases covered by rolled edge.

HABITAT: dry, exposed rock (not limestone).

SPORES: June-Sept.

Filmy Ferns *Hymenophyllaceae*

These tiniest of ferns, nearly all tropical, include species with fronds only half an inch long. With translucent leaves just one cell thick and lacking a protective epidermis, they require constant moisture and the deep shade of a rocky grotto.

SPORE CASES

Appalachian Bristle Fern
Trichomanes boschianum

SIZE: 2-6 in. long.

WHAT TO LOOK FOR: fronds lacy, thin, translucent, on creeping hairy rootstock; spore cases in cuplike structure with bristle.

HABITAT: deeply shaded recesses in moist sandstone cliffs; caves.

SPORES: Aug.-Oct.

Polypody Ferns *Polypodiaceae*

The leaves of these ferns are leathery and evergreen, a characteristic of plants growing where moisture is inconstant because of drought, winter winds, or local conditions. Most species live on rocks thinly covered with soil. Tropical members of this family usually grow on tree branches; the staghorn ferns (*Platycerium*) are often grown indoors on slabs of bark. Large round clusters of spore cases are typical of the group.

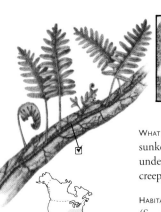

FERTILE LEAFLET

Resurrection Fern

Polypodium polypodioides

SIZE: 3-6 in. tall.

WHAT TO LOOK FOR: frond gray with scales below, green and with sunken midrib and raised dots above (from spore cases on underside); rolls up when dry, revives when wet; rootstock creeping, exposed.

HABITAT: rocks (northern part of range); tree trunks, branches (South). SPORES: July-Sept.

Common Polypody

Polypodium virginianum

SIZE:
4-10 in. tall.

WHAT TO LOOK FOR:
fronds evergreen, leathery, smooth; leaflets cut almost to stalk; rootstocks intertwined.

HABITAT:
shaded rocks in woods.

SPORES:
July-Sept.

Tree Ferns *Cyatheaceae*

These ferns of field and woodland are mostly medium to large, with spreading fronds much divided into leaflets and subleaflets. They include Bracken, one of the few ferns with worldwide distribution, and the tall tropical tree ferns (*Cyathea* and *Dicksonia*) cultivated in greenhouses and also outdoors along the California coast and in other warm places.

FERTILE SUBLEAFLET

Hay-scented Fern
Dennstaedtia punctilobula

SIZE: 15-35 in. tall.

WHAT TO LOOK FOR: fronds delicate, soft, yellow-green, with slightly sticky hairs; tip often arching; spore cases on edge of subleaflet, in cuplike structures; often grows in large colonies.

HABITAT: edges of fields, openings in woods; sandy soil.

SPORES: July-Oct.

Bracken
Pteridium aquilinum

SIZE: 2-3 ft. tall.

WHAT TO LOOK FOR: fronds broad, coarse, horizontal, triangular, usually divided into 3 large triangular leaflets; usually forms large colonies.

HABITAT: fields, brushy or burned-over areas, openings in woods; poor soils. SPORES: July-Aug. (often not formed).

Spleenworts *Aspleniaceae*

This is the most diverse fern family (some 3,000 species worldwide), and any generalization about habitat or appearance will have many exceptions. Spleenworts occur from the tropics to the Arctic; they range in size from the very large to the very small; their fronds may be undivided, finely divided, or somewhere in between. Closely related species within the family show a strong tendency to hybridize, sometimes producing intermediate forms that have their own names and reproduce like normal species. (The Lobed Spleenwort is one example.) The spleenwort family, so called because certain species could supposedly cure diseases of the spleen, includes all the ferns shown on this and the next 16 pages through the Toothed Wood Fern.

SPORE CASES

Hammock Fern

Thelypteris kunthii

SIZE:
2-5 ft. tall.

WHAT TO LOOK FOR:
fronds broad, with dense white hairs; lowest leaflets not reduced in size; edges not rolled over spore cases: veins unbranched.

HABITAT:
hammocks, low woods, rocky slopes.

SPORES:
May-Nov.

Long Beech Fern

Thelypteris phegopteris

SIZE:
10-20 in. tall.

WHAT TO LOOK FOR:
fronds arched, triangular, narrow, with "wings" connecting all but the lowest 2 pairs of leaflets; lowest leaflets drooping; stalks and undersides of leaflets hairy.

HABITAT:
damp rocky hillsides, cliffs, woods; often near streams.

SPORES:
July-Sept.

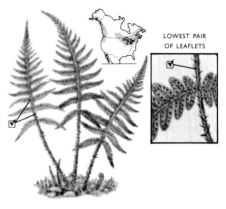

LOWEST PAIR
OF LEAFLETS

Broad Beech Fern

Thelypteris hexagonoptera

SIZE:
15-30 in. tall.

WHAT TO LOOK FOR:
fronds triangular, broad, with "wings" connecting all leaflets; leaflets with fine hairs on both surfaces.

HABITAT:
rich shaded woods.

SPORES:
July-Sept.

LOWEST PAIR

New York Fern

Thelypteris noveboracensis

SIZE:
15-25 in. tall.

WHAT TO LOOK FOR:
leaflets longest at center of frond; lowest leaflets tiny, triangular; spore cases near edge of subleaflet (edge not rolled over).

HABITAT:
moist woods, thickets; in sunny openings.

SPORES:
June-Sept.

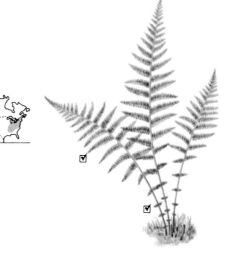

STERILE LEAFLET

Marsh Fern

Thelypteris palustris

SIZE:
15-30 in. tall.

WHAT TO LOOK FOR:
lowest pair of leaflets as long as, or slightly shorter than, next pair; fertile leaflets on taller fronds, with branched veins, rolled-over edges, and rows of spore cases not near edge.

HABITAT:
marshes, swamps, wet woods, wet meadows.

SPORES:
July-Sept.

FERTILE LEAFLET

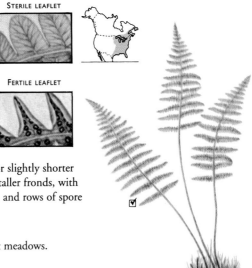

Wall Rue

Asplenium ruta-muraria

SIZE:
1½-6½ in. long.

WHAT TO LOOK FOR:
fronds dainty, triangular, with
stemmed leaflets and diamond-shaped, slightly toothed
subleaflets; spore cases dense, along veins.

HABITAT:
shaded limestone rocks; occasionally on old walls (in mortar).

SPORES:
June-Oct.

Maidenhair Spleenwort

Asplenium trichomanes

SIZE:
3-8 in. long.

FERTILE LEAFLET

WHAT TO LOOK FOR:
sterile fronds flat, spreading from center; fertile
fronds tall, with spore case clusters in crescents;
stalks stiff, purple-brown, shiny, persisting after
leaflets drop; leaflets oval, opposite, vaguely toothed.

HABITAT:
shaded rock crevices; usually in limestone.

SPORES:
June-Oct.

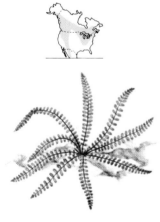

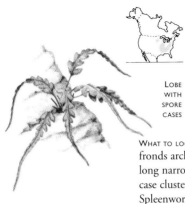

LOBE
WITH
SPORE
CASES

Lobed Spleenwort

Asplenosorus pinnatifidus

SIZE:
3-6 in. long.

WHAT TO LOOK FOR:
fronds arching to flat, spreading from center, leathery, with long narrow tip; lower half or more of frond lobed; spore case clusters in crescents along veins; hybrid of Mountain Spleenwort and Walking Fern.

HABITAT:
sandstone and other acidic rock cliffs.

SPORES:
June-Oct.

Ebony Spleenwort

Asplenium platyneuron

SIZE:
6-18 in. tall.

WHAT TO LOOK FOR:
fertile fronds erect; sterile fronds short, spreading; stalks shiny, dark brown; leaflets almost oblong, over-lapping stalk at base, with "ear" on upper edge; spore cases along veins, sometimes meeting at central vein.

HABITAT:
old field, woods, roadsides.

SPORES:
May-Nov.

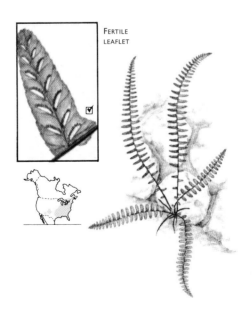

FERTILE
LEAFLET

Mountain Spleenwort

Asplenium montanum

SIZE:
3-7 in. long.

WHAT TO LOOK FOR:
fronds thick-textured, shiny green, twice divided, usually drooping; subleaflets with irregular edge; spore cases along veins.

HABITAT:
crevices in sandstone, quartzite, granite, or schist.

SPORES:
June-Oct.

Hart's-Tongue Fern

Phyllitis scolopendrium

SIZE:
6-12 in. long.

WHAT TO LOOK FOR:
fronds undivided, leathery, with heart-shaped base; spore cases in parallel rows along veins.

HABITAT:
mossy crevices in shaded limestone or dolomite outcrops.

SPORES:
July-Sept.

Walking Fern

Camptosorus rhizophyllus

SIZE: 4-12 in. long.

WHAT TO LOOK FOR: fronds arrow-shaped, undivided, arching (eventually flattening) with new plants at threadlike tips; spore cases scattered, along network of veins.

HABITAT: mossy rocks and cliffs, especially of limestone.

SPORES: July-Oct.

FERTILE FROND

Narrow-leaved Spleenwort

(Glade Fern) *Athyrium pycnocarpon*

SIZE: 1-2½ ft. tall.

WHAT TO LOOK FOR: sterile fronds slightly arching, with thin, unlobed leaflets; fertile fronds taller, straight, with smaller, more widely separated leaflets; stalks green, without long hairs; spore cases in closely spaced lines along veins.

HABITAT: rich woods, rocky hillsides, ravines.

SPORES: Aug.-Oct.

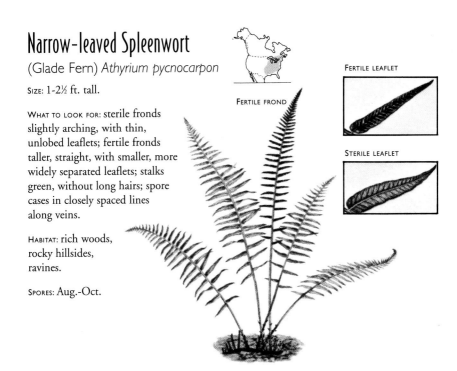

FERTILE FROND

FERTILE LEAFLET

STERILE LEAFLET

Lady Fern

Athyrium filix-femina

SIZE:
1-3 ft. tall.

WHAT TO LOOK FOR:
fronds delicate, finely cut, with drooping tip and minutely toothed subleaflets; stalk smooth, easily broken, with 2 strands inside; spore cases short, tightly curved.

HABITAT:
rich woods, swamps.

SPORES:
July-Aug.

FERTILE SUBLEAFLET

Silvery Glade Fern

Athyrium thelypterioides

SIZE:
1½-3 ft. tall.

WHAT TO LOOK FOR:
leaflets firm-textured, shorter near base, deeply cut (but not to midvein); lowest pair hangs down; long pale hairs on undersides, stalks, and midribs; spore case clusters mostly long, straight, silvery when young.

HABITAT:
rich, damp woods.

SPORES:
July-Sept.

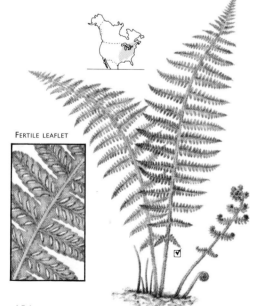

FERTILE LEAFLET

Bulblet Fern

Cystopteris bulbifera

SIZE:
10-20 in. long.

WHAT TO LOOK FOR:
fronds widest at base, drooping at tip; leaflets widely spaced, with 1 or more round bulbs (bulbs fall off and grow); stalks and midribs green-pink; spore cases sparse.

HABITAT:
shaded limestone cliffs; white-cedar or hardwood swamps.

SPORES:
June-Aug.

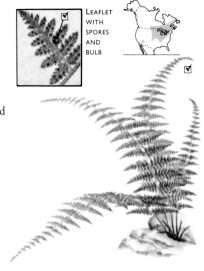

LEAFLET WITH SPORES AND BULB

FERTILE LEAFLET

Fragile Fern

(Brittle Fern)

Cystopteris fragilis

SIZE:
6-12 in. tall.

WHAT TO LOOK FOR:
fronds erect, widest at center, often dying in summer and then growing back; leaflets thin, widely spaced, once or twice divided; stalks hairless, dark near base, green above, easily broken; spore cases sparse.

HABITAT:
rocks; occasionally in woodland soil.

SPORES:
May-Aug.

Blunt-lobed Woodsia

Woodsia obtusa

SIZE:
10-20 in. tall.

WHAT TO LOOK FOR:
stalks not jointed; leaflets widely spaced; stalk and underside of frond with a few delicate, pale tan scales; spore cases scaly.

HABITAT:
boulders; rocky slopes and woods.

SPORES:
July-Oct.

FERTILE LEAFLET

Rusty Woodsia

Woodsia ilvensis

SIZE:
5-15 in. tall.

WHAT TO LOOK FOR:
stalk with 1 joint, hairy, scaly; stubble of uniform height (stalk breaks at joint); leaflets hairy and white (turning rusty) below; spore cases, hairy near edge of leaflet.

HABITAT:
rocky slopes, ledges.

SPORES:
July-Oct.

FERTILE LEAFLET

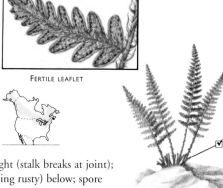

Mountain Woodsia

Woodsia scopulina

SIZE:
5-15 in. tall.

WHAT TO LOOK FOR:
stalks not jointed; no stubble; stalks
and undersides of fronds scaleless,
with scattered white hairs; spore
cases hairy.

HABITAT:
cliffs, talus slopes.

SPORES:
July-Oct.

FERTILE LEAFLET

FERTILE LEAFLET

Western Woodsia

Woodsia oregana

SIZE:
5-15 in. tall.

WHAT TO LOOK FOR:
stalks not jointed, brown near base and yellow above; no stubble;
stalks and undersides of fronds scaleless, without white hairs; spore
cases hairy.

HABITAT:
cliffs, talus slopes.

SPORES:
July-Oct.

Northern Holly Fern

Polystichum lonchitis

SIZE:
6-18 in. tall.

WHAT TO LOOK FOR:
fronds shiny, dark green, tapering at tip and base; leaflets pointed, bristle-toothed, with "ear"; stalks scaly; spore cases usually in 2 rows.

HABITAT:
rocky forests, especially in mountains.

SPORES:
July-Sept.

FERTILE LEAFLET

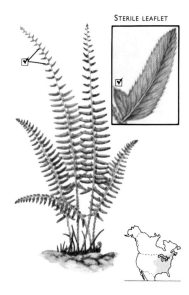

STERILE LEAFLET

Christmas Fern

Polystichum acrostichoides

SIZE:
12-30 in. tall.

WHAT TO LOOK FOR:
fronds evergreen, thick; leaflets pointed, minutely toothed, with "ear"; stalks scaly; fertile leaflets smaller, near tip, with 2 rows of spore cases.

HABITAT:
woods, streambanks.

SPORES:
June-Oct.

Western Sword Fern

Polystichum munitum

SIZE:
20-50 in. tall.

WHAT TO LOOK FOR:
fronds erect, evergreen, tapering slightly near base; leaflets bristle-toothed, with "ear"; fertile leaflets similar to sterile; stalks with large and small scales; spore cases in 2 or more rows.

HABITAT:
forests, rocky slopes; usually in shade.

SPORES:
May-Aug.

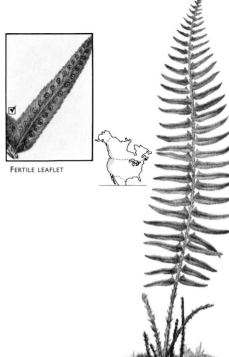

FERTILE LEAFLET

Sensitive Fern

Onoclea sensibilis

SIZE:
15-30 in. tall.

WHAT TO LOOK FOR:
sterile fronds finely veined, divided on lower portion and lobed toward tip; fertile fronds brown, beaded, conspicuous in winter.

HABITAT:
wet ground, marshes, swamps.

SPORES:
Mar.-May.

Ostrich Fern

Matteuccia struthiopteris

SIZE:
2-6 ft. tall.

WHAT TO LOOK FOR:
vase-shaped clump; sterile fronds plume-like, widest above midpoint, with deeply lobed leaflets; fertile fronds shorter, hard, brown and erect in winter.

HABITAT:
damp woods, swamps, streambanks.

SPORES:
Apr.-June.

Male Fern

Dryopteris filix-mas

SIZE:
15-30 in. tall.

WHAT TO LOOK FOR:
fronds lance-shaped, tapering
toward base; stalks densely scaled; leaflets thin; spore
case clusters kidney-shaped, between center vein and
edge.

HABITAT:
rocky slopes, rich forests.

SPORES:
July-Sept.

FERTILE SUBLEAFLET

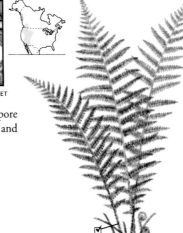

Goldie's Wood Fern

Dryopteris goldiana

SIZE:
2-4 ft. tall.

WHAT TO LOOK FOR:
fronds very broad, narrowing abruptly
at tip; stalks scaly, especially at base;
leaflets deeply cut, widest at midpoint;
spore case clusters kidney-shaped, not
crowded.

HABITAT:
rich, damp woods.

SPORES:
July-Oct.

BASE OF FERTILE
LEAFLETS

Nonflowering Plants 161

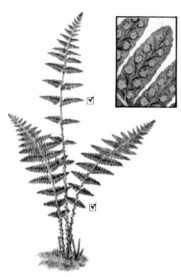

FERTILE
LEAFLET

Crested Wood Fern

Dryopteris cristata

SIZE:
1½-3 ft. tall.

WHAT TO LOOK FOR:
fronds narrow; fertile fronds erect, with horizontal leaflets; sterile fronds shorter, spreading, evergreen; lower leaflets smaller, more triangular; spore case clusters kidney-shaped, crowded.

HABITAT:
swamps, marshes, damp woods.

SPORES:
June-Sept.

Marginal Wood Fern

Dryopteris marginalis

SIZE:
15-40 in. tall.

FERTILE SUBLEAFLET

WHAT TO LOOK FOR:
fronds lance-shaped, evergreen, not tapering toward base; stalks scaly, especially at base; leaflets thick, dark blue-green, curving up at tip; spore case clusters kidney-shaped, at edges of subleaflet.

HABITAT:
forests, rocky slopes, swamps.

SPORES:
June-Oct.

FERTILE
SUBLEAFLET

Toothed Wood Fern

Dryopteris carthusiana

SIZE:
1½-3 ft. tall.

WHAT TO LOOK FOR:
fronds very lacy, arching; leaflets triangular; stalks scaly; first downward-pointing subleaflet on lowest leaflets usually longer than its opposite; spore case clusters kidney-shaped.

HABITAT:
swamps, marshes, damp woods.

SPORES:
July-Oct.

Deer Fern

Blechnum spicant

SIZE
1-3 ft. tall:

WHAT TO LOOK FOR:
sterile fronds short, evergreen, spreading, cut almost to stalk; fertile fronds tall, erect, with narrow, widely spaced divisions; spore cases extend from base to tip of fertile "leaflet."

HABITAT:
damp, shaded slopes, especially in coniferous forests.

SPORES:
July-Sept.

SPORE CASES   FERTILE FROND

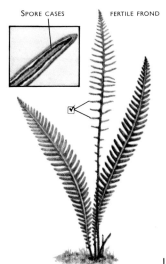

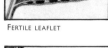

FERTILE LEAFLET

STERILE LEAFLET

Netted Chain Fern

Woodwardia areolata

SIZE: 1½-3½ ft. tall.

WHAT TO LOOK FOR: fronds with unpaired leaflets, mostly not cut to stalk; leaflets with netlike veins; sterile fronds dark green; fertile fronds more erect, with narrow leaflets and 2 chainlike rows of spore cases.

HABITAT: bogs, swamps.

SPORES: July-Oct.

FERTILE LEAFLET   **STERILE LEAFLET**

Virginia Chain Fern

Woodwardia virginica

SIZE: 2-4 ft. tall.

WHAT TO LOOK FOR: fronds resembling Cinnamon Fern's but not clumped; row of netted veins; spore cases beside veins, forming chains; stalks shiny, dark purple-brown.

HABITAT: swamps, bogs, wet spots in woods.

SPORES: July-Sept.

FERTILE LOBE

Oak Fern

Gymnocarpium dryopteris

SIZE:
5-15 in. tall.

WHAT TO LOOK FOR:
fronds delicate, horizontal, triangular in outline (often with 3 leaflets); lower leaflets triangular; spore case clusters minute, round.

HABITAT:
cool woods, rocky slopes.

SPORES:
July-Sept.

Giant Chain Fern

Woodwardia fimbriata

SIZE:
4-6 ft. tall.

WHAT TO LOOK FOR:
fronds huge, oblong, clustered; leaflets deeply cut;
spore case clusters long, close to midvein.

HABITAT:
seepage areas in foothills, mountains.

SPORES:
May-Aug.

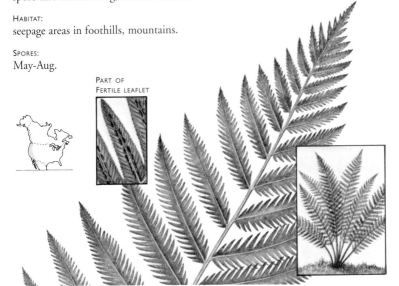

PART OF
FERTILE LEAFLET

Water Spangles *Salviniaceae*

These peculiar floating ferns, seemingly so tender, become menacing pests when they invade and choke reservoirs. The rootlike masses that hang down in the water are really leaves of a special kind, with round, spore-containing sacs.

Water Spangles
Salvinia minima

SIZE: leaves ¾-1 in. long.

WHAT TO LOOK FOR: floating leaves nearly round, hairy above, usually reddish below; spores under leaves, in globular sacs, hanging in water.

HABITAT: ponds, reservoirs, other still-water areas.

SPORES: July-Oct.

LEAVES AND
SPORE SACS

Mosquito Ferns *Azollaceae*

The connection between mosquito ferns and mosquitoes, some say, is that these aquatic plants stifle mosquito growth. In Asian rice paddies, nitrogen-fixing algae living in their leaves serve to maintain the fertility of the soil. Species microscopically different from the one shown grow in parts of the American West and Midwest.

Mosquito Fern
Azolla caroliniana

SIZE: leaves to ¹⁄₁₀ in. long.

LEAVES

WHAT TO LOOK FOR: masses of floating plants; leaves gray-green (in shade) or reddish (sun), with upper and lower lobes, in 2 overlapping rows.

HABITAT: ponds, slow streams, bayous.

SPORES: June-Sept.

Water Clovers *Marsileaceae*

Adapted to dry prairies, these unfernlike ferns appear in ponds after spring rains. They go through their life cycle in just a few weeks, starting out as fiddleheads and unrolling like a typical fern. Generally, their cordlike stems are anchored in the mud.

Hairy Water Clover

Marsilea vestita

SIZE: 3-6 in. tall.

WHAT TO LOOK FOR: floating fronds resembling 4-leaved clovers; spore cases hard, nutlike, at base of stalk.

HABITAT: ditches, meadows, shores of rivers and ponds.

SPORES: May-Sept.

Club-mosses *Lycopodiaceae*

Their names belying their position in the plant world, the Running Cedar, or Ground Pine, and other clubmosses are neither low-growing conifers nor types of moss. These delightful evergreens, with their dense, narrow, single-veined leaves, are closely related to horsetails and ferns. Clubmosses propagate mainly by creeping along the ground, for their spores, usually produced in distinct "cones" (the "clubs"), germinate rarely or not at all. Some species also produce new plants—"plantlets"—on their leaves.

Shining Club-moss

Lycopodium lucidulum

SIZE: 3-6 in. tall.

WHAT TO LOOK FOR: upright branching stems; shiny, dark green, delicately toothed leaves; spore cases orange-yellow, at bases of upper leaves; flat, green plantlets on upper leaves.

HABITAT: moist woods.

SPORES: Sept.-Oct.

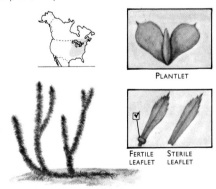

PLANTLET

FERTILE LEAFLET   STERILE LEAFLET

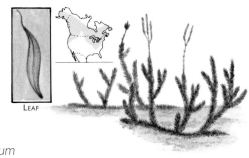

Running Cedar

(Ground Pine)

Lycopodium clavatum

SIZE: 4-10 in. tall.

WHAT TO LOOK FOR: creeping horizontal stems and branching upright stems; narrow leaves tapering to single hair at tip; fertile shoots taller, with spores in clusters of "cones."

HABITAT: woods, brushy areas; in sandy soils.

SPORES: Sept.-Oct.

LEAF

Bog Club-moss

Lycopodium inundatum

SIZE: 3-4 in. tall.

WHAT TO LOOK FOR: creeping horizontal stems and unbranched upright stems; narrow, soft, pale green leaves (not evergreen); spores in bushy "cones."

HABITAT: bogs, sandy marshes, ditches, pine barrens, pond edges.

SPORES: Sept.-Oct.

Running Pine

Lycopodium digitatum

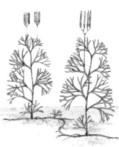

BRANCHLET

SIZE:
5-10 in. tall.

WHAT TO LOOK FOR:
upright stems with flat, fanlike branchlets; long horizontal stems on ground or below leaf litter; leaves small, leathery, flat, with pointed tip, in 4 rows; spores in "cones" at top of taller branched stems.

HABITAT:
dry, upland second-growth woods; in acid soils.

SPORES:
Sept.-Oct.

Tree Club-moss

Lycopodium obscurum

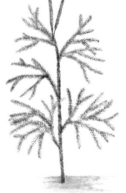

BRANCHLET

SIZE:
4-7 in. tall.

WHAT TO LOOK FOR:
treelike form, branching several times; branches slightly flattened, with very narrow leaves; fertile shoots at top of plant, with spores in clusters of "cones."

HABITAT:
woods, bogs.

SPORES:
Aug.-Oct.

Spike-mosses *Selaginellaceae*

Small and delicate, these plants are easily mistaken for mosses or club-mosses. They form mats or tufts with upright branches rising from creeping, threadlike stems. Minute overlapping leaflets clothe the stems. Some of the branch tips are sterile, others fertile, the latter generally bearing four-sided "cones." One of the strangest spike-mosses is the Resurrection Plant (*Selaginella lepidophylla*) of southern Texas and Mexico, often sold as a novelty. When dry, it curls into a tight ball; watered, it opens out flat

Meadow Spike-moss

Selaginella apoda

SIZE:
1 in. tall.

WHAT TO LOOK FOR:
pale green creeping plant with 2 types of leaves (tiny ones in 2 rows along top of stem, larger flat ones on each side); spores in 4-sided cones at tips of branches.

HABITAT:
wet rock seeps, damp meadows; marshes (in tufts of sedges).

SPORES:
July-Sept.

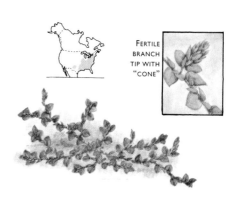

FERTILE BRANCH TIP WITH "CONE"

Rock Spike-moss

Selaginella rupestris

SIZE:
1-3 in. tall.

WHAT TO LOOK FOR:
horizontal and upright stems with rather widely spaced branches; sterile leaves narrow, with hairy edges and pointed tip; fertile branches 4-sided, with wider leaves.

HABITAT:
rocks; soil in dry, sandy woods.

SPORES:
Aug.-Sept. (often at other times).

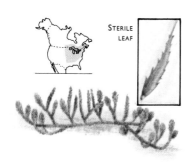

STERILE LEAF

Rocky Mountain Spike-moss

Selaginella densa

Size: ½-1½ in. tall.

WHAT TO LOOK FOR:
tight masses of compact, dense branches; leaves narrow, with tiny hairs on edges and a pointed tip.

HABITAT:
sagebrush flats, deserts; dry, rocky slopes; alpine meadows.

SPORES:
Aug.-Sept. (often at other times).

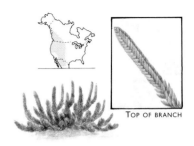

TOP OF BRANCH

Quillworts *Isoetaceae*

Though quillworts look remarkably like grass (they are sometimes called Merlin's grass), they have spores rather than seeds and are close allies of ferns. Spanning the continent, the group is generally associated with water; quillworts grow in northern and alpine lakes and in temporary ponds on prairies and among rocks. Most have "bulbs" at the base.

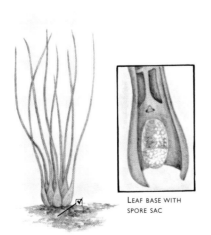

LEAF BASE WITH
SPORE SAC

Spiny-spored Quillwort

Isoetes echinospora

SIZE:
3-15 in. tall.

WHAT TO LOOK FOR:
bulblike base; leaves resembling grass or chives, appearing jointed; leaf base wide, rounded, with sac holding spores; spores look like sugar granules.

HABITAT:
in ponds or lakes or on shore.

SPORES:
June-Oct.

Horsetails *Equisetaceae*

Hundreds of millions of years ago the spore-bearing horsetails dominated much of the earth, but over the ages, seed-producing plants have usurped their position. Horsetails are easy to recognize: their stems are jointed and ridged, and portions may feel gritty to the touch. The stems of most species have a hollow central canal surrounded by smaller cavities. Horsetails thrive in damp places. The unbranched types, called scouring rushes, were once used for cleaning pots and pans.

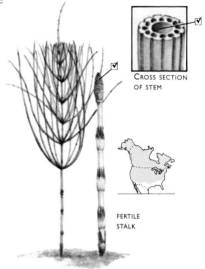

CROSS SECTION OF STEM

Field Horsetail
Equisetum arvense

SIZE: 1-2½ ft. tall.

WHAT TO LOOK FOR: coarse plants; whorls of branches at joints; relatively small central canal; spores in cone on separate, short-lived, pink-brown stalk.

HABITAT: woods, fields, swamps, railroad embankments, roadsides, waste places.

SPORES: Mar.-May.

FERTILE STALK

Smooth Scouring-rush
Equisetum laevigatum

SIZE: 1-2 ft. tall.

WHAT TO LOOK FOR: smooth, stiff stem (dies in winter); large central canal; spore "cone" usually rounded at top.

HABITAT: dry fields, prairies, edges of ditches and marshes.

SPORES: July-Aug.

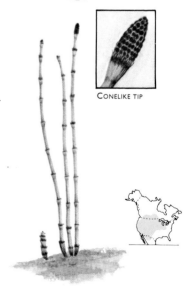

CONELIKE TIP

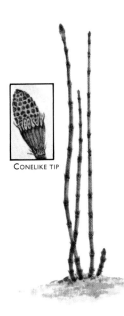

CONELIKE TIP

Scouring-rush

Equisetum hyemale

SIZE:
1½-2½ ft. tall.

WHAT TO LOOK FOR:
stiff, hard, rough stem, unbranched except when injured; large central canal; spores in "cone" with strong prickle.

HABITAT:
roadsides, lakeshores, floodplains.

SPORES:
Apr.-June (often at other times).

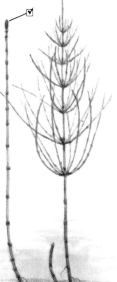

Water Horsetail

(Pipes)

Equisetum fluviatile

SIZE:
2-3 ft. tall.

WHAT TO LOOK FOR:
delicate, thin, soft stem, usually with branches; very large central canal; spores in "cone."

HABITAT:
swamps, marshes, ponds, ditches.

SPORES:
June-Aug.

Mosses *Musci*

Plants popularly known as mosses run the gamut from such flowering species as Spanish moss to algae (Sea Moss) and lichens (Reindeer Moss). In the scientific sense, however, mosses include only certain "lower" plants—lower not because they grow close to the ground (though indeed they do) but because they lack the water-carrying pipelines of ferns and flowering plants. True mosses have a complex life cycle that includes spores rather than seeds. The spores are generally produced at the end of a long stalk, in a covered case whose lid falls off when the spores are mature. Many species can be distinguished from closely related look-alikes only by microscopic examination of their spore cases or leaves.

Water Fern Moss
Fissidens grandifrons

SIZE:
2-4 in. tall.

WHAT TO LOOK FOR:
coarse, rigid, dark blue-green plants; leaves in 2 rows, clasping stems, with midrib; leaf base clasps leaf above; spore cases rare.

HABITAT:
running water; on limestone.

PLANTS GROWING IN STREAM

GROWTH FORM

White Cushion Moss
Leucobryum glaucum

SIZE:
2-4 in. tall.

WHAT TO LOOK FOR:
dense white cushion (blue-green when wet); leaves thick, very narrow, crowded on stem; spore cases rare.

HABITAT:
moist woods; on soil or very decayed wood.

Red Spoonleaf Peat Moss

Sphagnum magellanicum

SIZE:
6-8 in. tall.

WHAT TO LOOK FOR:
spongy, shiny red cushion (pink-green in shade); branches fat, bunched, spreading or drooping, forming rosette at top; leaves round-tipped, overlapping, very concave; spore cases rare.

HABITAT:
bogs; usually in sun.

PLANT WITH
SPORE CASE

Burned Ground Moss

(Purple Moss)

Ceratodon purpureus

SIZE:
to 1 in. tall.

WHAT TO LOOK FOR:
dense velvety green tuft (brown when dry); leaves narrow, with edges rolled under the midrib that ends with short red bristle; stems and spore cases purple-red; spore case horizontal, furrowed, with cone-shaped lid.

HABITAT:
dry, disturbed places; roadsides, fields, roofs.

Cord Moss

Funaria hygrometrica

Size: ½ in. tall.

What to look for: loose, pale yellow-green mat; spore cases numerous, large, asymmetrical, held horizontal or hanging from long, twisted, curled stalk.

Habitat: disturbed places, especially on bare soil and burns; greenhouse pots.

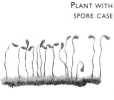

PLANT WITH
SPORE CASE

Broom Moss

Dicranum scoparium

Size:
2-4 in. tall.

What to look for:
stems upright, with leaves turned in one direction (looks windswept); leaves narrow, with midrib extending to tip; spore case curved, with beaked lid, at about right angle to stem.

Habitat:
woods; on soil or leaf litter.

Rock Moss

Grimmia alpicola

Size:
1 in. tall.

What to look for:
rigid plants in small cushion or tuft, green (wet) or blackish (dry); upper leaves erect, nearly hiding spore case; spore case with fringe of red teeth at mouth.

Habitat:
exposed places, mountains; on dry limestone rocks.

SPORE CASE

Tree Moss

Climacium dendroides

SIZE:
2-4 in. tall.

WHAT TO LOOK FOR:
erect, much-branching stems (resemble little trees),
yellow- to dark green; leaves broad, pressed close on
stem, narrower and spreading on branches; creeping
underground stem; spore cases rare.

HABITAT:
swampy areas; on wet humus, decaying wood.

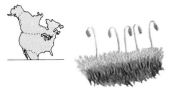

SPORE
CASE

Silver Moss

Bryum argenteum

SIZE:
½ in. tall.

WHAT TO LOOK FOR:
dense, shiny, silver-green cushion of branching plants; leaves broadly
oval, tapering abruptly, overlapping, pressed close to stem, with midrib
ending before tip; spore case red, hanging, with short-pointed lid.

HABITAT:
roadsides, sidewalks, roofs, fields, other waste places.

Woodsy Mnium

(Star Moss) *Mnium cuspidatum*

SIZE: 1-½ in. tall.

WHAT TO LOOK FOR: erect stems with oval leaves crowded at top (smaller at base); creeping stems (not shown) with leaves in 2 rows; spore case nodding, with short-pointed lid, on erect stem.

HABITAT: woods, fields, lawns, roadsides; in shade.

Delicate Fern Moss

Thuidium delicatulum

SIZE:
2-4 in. long.

WHAT TO LOOK FOR:
feathery, much-branching mat; leaves on main stem tapered from oval base, pressed close to stem, larger than branch leaves; spore cases not abundant.

HABITAT:
woods; on moist or wet soil, leaf litter, decaying wood.

Haircap Moss

(Goldilocks) *Polytrichum commune*

SIZE: 6-12 in. tall.

WHAT TO LOOK FOR: tall, wiry plants; leaves slender, toothed, held straight out (pressed to stem when dry) with long green ridges on upper surface; 4-sided spore case (covered by hairy hood until mature), at top of long stalk; plants without spore cases may have yellow "flower buds."

HABITAT: woods, edges of bogs.

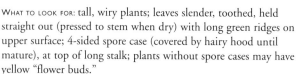

Spineleaf Moss

Atrichum undulatum

SIZE: 1-2½ in. tall.

MATURE
SPORE CASE

WHAT TO LOOK FOR: leaves narrow, wavy, with narrow midrib covered by several green ridges; green (brown and very curled when dry) spore case curved, slightly tilted, long-stalked, with beaked lid until mature.

HABITAT: moist woods; on disturbed soil, especially streambanks and uprooted trees.

Four-tooth Moss

Tetraphis pellucida

SIZE: ½ in. tall.

STERILE
PLANT

MATURE
SPORE CASE

WHAT TO LOOK FOR: dense tuft of upright stems; leaves elliptical, with midrib to tip; plants without spore cases topped by leafy cup; spore case erect, on long stalk, with 4 narrow triangular teeth at open end.

HABITAT: swamps, woods; on decaying wood, in soil.

Feather Moss

Hypnum imponens

SIZE: 2-4 in. long.

WHAT TO LOOK FOR: soft, featherlike, branching, prostrate plants; leaves curled downward; spore case almost upright, on long stalk.

HABITAT: swamps, coniferous woods; on decaying logs, on humus, at base of trees.

Liverworts and Hornworts *Hepaticae and Anthocerotae*

Liverworts and hornworts lead mosslike lives, and in many species the spore-producing capsule looks much like that of a moss without the lid. Liverworts often reproduce by means of little green buds, called gemmae. The plants take their name—and their reputation as a cure for liver disease—from the flat, liverlike shape of certain species.

Common Liverwort

Marchantia polymorpha

SIZE:
2-3 in. wide.

WHAT TO LOOK FOR:
leathery, dark green, branching ribbons; upper surface with diamond-shaped marks and small cuplike structures containing minute buds (gemmae); umbrella-shaped branches.

HABITAT:
moist, bare ground; wet woods, campfire sites, greenhouses, gardens.

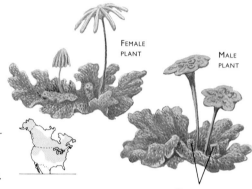

FEMALE PLANT

MALE PLANT

GEMMAE CUPS

Common Hornwort

Anthoceros laevis

SIZE:
½ in. wide.

WHAT TO LOOK FOR:
flat, dark green disk with scalloped edge; spores produced in erect, yellow-green "horn" that splits at tip, exposing slim central column.

HABITAT:
disturbed places; bare, moist clay; roadsides, fallow fields.

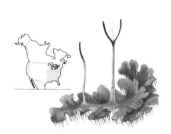

Fringed Waterwort

Ricciocarpus natans

SIZE:
½ in. wide.

WHAT TO LOOK FOR:
floating green plants; flat, fan- or
heart-shaped; edges shallowly lobed,
with dark purple hairlike scales;
forked channels corresponding to lobed
sections; reproductive structures buried.

HABITAT:
marshes, stream backwaters, puddles; stranded on mud.

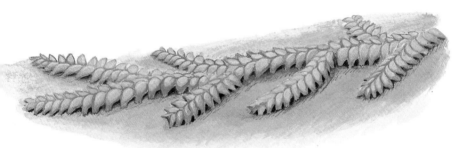

Braided Liverwort

Bazzania trilobata

UNDERSIDE
OF STEM

SIZE:
4-6 in. long.

WHAT TO LOOK FOR:
stem prostrate, forked into equal branches (a series of Y's); leaves
in 2 rows, overlapping, dark green, 3-toothed at rounded tip;
underside with small, toothed leaves and (occasionally) rootlets;
rarely fruiting.

HABITAT:
moist coniferous forests; old stumps, peaty banks, rocks.

Seaweeds

Part of the diverse assemblage of water-loving plants called algae, sea-weeds generally grow attached to rocks, shells, or other objects. Most frequently encountered in tidal areas, they range from the shore to depths of 100 feet or more (they must have light for photosynthesis). Species known as green seaweeds use the green pigment chlorophyll for photosynthesis; so do the red and the brown seaweeds, but they have other pigments that mask the presence of the green. Seaweeds lack true roots, stems, and leaves. They reproduce asexually by spores or sexually by the fusion of cells called gametes.

Tube Algae *Siphonales*

Most of these green algae (and related forms, too) grow in warm waters, where they gradually develop a crust of lime. Such is the case with the Mermaid's Wineglass (*Acetabularia crenulata*) and the Merman's Shaving Brush (*Penicillus capitatus*), whose names describe their appearance with accuracy as well as fantasy. Both species occur in calm seas off Florida; the Wineglass ranges west to Texas.

Sea Moss
Bryopsis corticulans

SIZE:
3-8 in. tall.

WHAT TO LOOK FOR:
clumps of fernlike seaweed; glossy, dark green; branches usually opposite.

HABITAT:
rocks swept by heavy surf.

Green Thread Algae *Ulotrichales*

Sea Lettuce and seaweeds similar to it grow from the tropics to the Arctic, but most of the other species in this group are inconspicuous freshwater plants. Each plant is divided into individual cells, each surrounded by a wall of cellulose. (Plants in the tube algae group have no cell walls.) The cell wall and other characteristics suggest that plants more complex than algae may have developed from ancestors such as these.

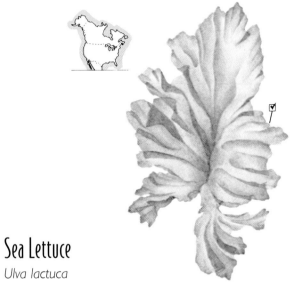

Sea Lettuce

Ulva lactuca

SIZE:
to 2 ft. long and wide.

WHAT TO LOOK FOR:
thin, medium green, lettucelike sheet; plain or ruffled edges; no stem.

HABITAT:
rocks or mud flats, estuaries or tidal areas.

Cartilaginous Red Algae *Gigartinales*

This large group of red seaweeds contains a number of conspicuous and commercially valuable species. Irish Moss, native to both sides of the Atlantic, is the source of carrageenan (carrageen), used in ice cream, yogurt, and certain other foods as a stabilizer and emulsifier; extracts of the plant can be used in milk puddings and fruit jellies. Irish Moss, Tufted Red Weed, and their West Coast relatives often grow abundantly on rocks exposed at low tide.

Irish Moss

Chondrus crispus

SIZE:
2-6 in. tall.

WHAT TO LOOK FOR:
clumps of multibranched seaweed;
dark purple-green, red-purple, or yellow; tough, leathery.

HABITAT:
tide pools, rock ledges, deeper waters.

Tufted Red Weed

Gigartina stellata

SIZE:
2-6 in. tall.

WHAT TO LOOK FOR:
dark red-purple or brownish
clump, with few branches; knobby growths on broad surfaces.

HABITAT:
lower tide pools, surf-swept rocks.

Wormlike Red Algae *Nemalionales*

Though seaweed botany may seem esoteric, its importance should not be underrated. Consider the cell walls of these and other red algae, which contain gelatinous substances extremely resistant to digestion. Since they are indigestible by man (and therefore noncaloric), manufacturers use them in diet foods. Indigestible by nearly all bacteria too, they furnish an excellent medium, called agar, for growing bacteria in the laboratory.

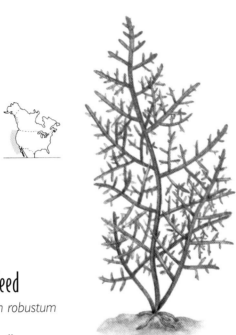

Agar Weed

Gelidium robustum

SIZE:
4-16 in. tall.

WHAT TO LOOK FOR:
bushy, erect, deep red plant; stem and branches somewhat flattened; tough but pliable.

HABITAT:
rocks; lower tidal zone and deeper.

Bang's Primitive Red Algae *Bangiales*

The several species called laver look fragile and shrink markedly when they dry out between tides, but they are surprisingly strong and resistant to tearing. High in protein and iodine, they can be eaten raw or cooked and are used as a food or condiment in the Orient and other places. A Japanese species is one of the few seaweeds that have been cultivated.

Laver

Porphyra perforata

SIZE: 6-12 in. long.

WHAT TO LOOK FOR: soft, slippery, tissue-thin sheet, variable in color (gray-pink to purple-red or gray-green); ruffled edges.

HABITAT: rocks or on other algae; upper or middle tidal zone.

Rosy-bladed Red Algae *Rhodymeniales*

Munching on Dulse is a custom—and an acquired taste—dating from the Middle Ages in northern Europe. Closely related species on the West Coast look much like Dulse; other members of the group are inflated and resemble bunches of grapes or fingers on a glove.

Dulse

(Neptune's Girdle)
Rhodymenia palmata

SIZE: 12-20 in. tall.

WHAT TO LOOK FOR: broad-bladed plant, with one blade or several (may have tiny blades along edges); red-purple, leathery.

HABITAT: rocks, shells, on larger algae; tidal areas.

Vesselled Red Algae *Ceramiales*

Chenille Weed is an oddity in this group, whose members are mainly small and inconspicuous. Large, feathery, and dramatically colored, it is a favorite for gluing onto paper and making seaweed pictures. Many vesselled red algae have a regular and delicate structure, noticeable when their branches are viewed through a hand lens or microscope.

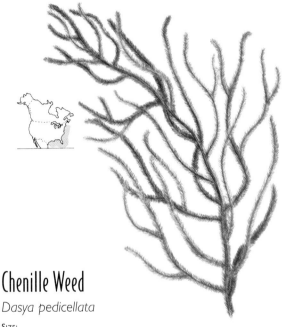

Chenille Weed

Dasya pedicellata

SIZE:
3-30 in. tall.

WHAT TO LOOK FOR:
branches few to many, slender, round, with delicate hairs; light to deep red-purple.

HABITAT:
shells, small stones; quiet shallow waters below low-tide line.

Kelps *Laminariales*

The most conspicuous brown seaweeds on either coast are the kelps, a group that includes some of the world's largest plants. They have a rather elaborate structure for seaweeds: all but the Smooth Cord Weed have a cylindrical stem, one or more flattened blades, and a specialized holdfast attached to rocks or other solid objects. Kelps reproduce by shedding millions of microscopic spores, which develop into microscopic plantlets. From these plantlets come free-floating gametes, which once united (no mean feat in the open ocean), grow rapidly into mature plants. Some of the largest species, such as the Bull Kelp, attain full size, reproduce, and die within a year.

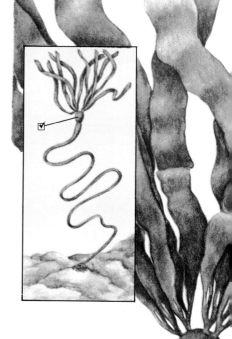

Bull Kelp

Nereocystis luetkeana

SIZE:
to 130 ft. long; stem to 115 ft. long.

WHAT TO LOOK FOR:
many floating brown blades coming from stem; bulblike bladder where blades join stem.

HABITAT:
rocks; deep water.

Smooth Cord Weed
Chorda filum

SIZE: to 15 ft. long.

WHAT TO LOOK FOR: slender, brown, unbranched cords nearly reaching surface; lower part hollow.

HABITAT: stones, shells; near and below low-tide line in sheltered locations.

Sugar Wrack
Laminaria saccharina

SIZE: to 15 ft. long.

WHAT TO LOOK FOR: single wide olive-brown blade; ruffled edges (summer); white powder on surface when dry; tough stem; branched holdfast.

HABITAT: rocks below low-tide line.

Sea Palm
Postelsia palmaeformis

SIZE: 1-2 ft. tall; blades 6-10 in. long.

WHAT TO LOOK FOR: olive-brown seaweed resembling miniature palm tree; stem hollow, flexible, remaining upright when water recedes; in large stands.

HABITAT: surf-swept rocks.

Giant Kelp
Macrocystis pyrifera

SIZE:
to 230 ft. long;
blades 10-30 in. long.

WHAT TO LOOK FOR:
brown seaweed with long main stem and leaf-shaped blades on side stems; hollow bladder at base of blade; leaf-shaped blades split off from semicircular blade at tip.

HABITAT:
rocks, coarse sand; deep water.

Rockweeds *Fucales*

These are the most advanced brown seaweeds in terms of reproduction. Instead of shedding free-floating spores, as the kelps do, they produce their reproductive cells (gametes) in special, usually swollen, branch tips. As the tide goes out and the tips shrink, the ripe gametes are squeezed out in drops of mucilage. The returning tide sweeps up the gametes, concentrating them and enhancing the chances for successful union. Seaweeds in this group typically live for more than a year; Rockweed and close relatives have a life span of about three years. The group has a wide range on both coasts.

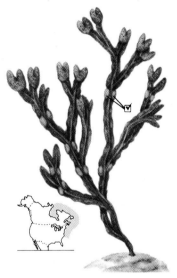

Rockweed

Fucus vesiculosus

SIZE: 4-36 in. tall.

WHAT TO LOOK FOR: olive-brown, mucilaginous seaweed; stems flattened with raised midrib, branching repeatedly in Y shape; may have paired oval bladders on sides of midrib.

HABITAT: boulders, ledges; tidal areas.

Attached Gulfweed

Sargassum filipendula

SIZE: 6-36 in. tall.

WHAT TO LOOK FOR: light or yellowish-brown seaweed with few to many branches; leafy blades with toothed edges; berrylike bladders on short stems.

HABITAT: rocks, shells; at or below low-tide line.

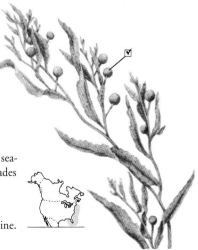

Lichens *Lichenes*

Thriving under such stressful conditions as extreme cold and drought, lichens have the remarkable ability to grow where few other plants can—on rocks and tombstones, in deserts and in the Far North. Even more amazing is just what they are: unique combinations of two distinct species, an alga (a primitive aquatic plant) and a fungus. The algae, which can photosynthesize, contribute food; the fungi, it is believed, furnish water and shade.

Reproduction might seem a problem for such partnership plants. In many cases small bits break off and grow into new lichens. Sometimes the fungus produces spores that are released along with a few algal cells. Or wind-blown spores from the fungus may come into contact with free-living algae and develop with them into lichen.

People living in places where lichens are common have found many a use for these curious plants. Boiled in water, they yield fabric dyes used most notably by Scots in coloring Harris tweeds. Some furnish smoking materials, some medicine. Though the Wolf Lichen was reputedly used as an Old World wolf-killer, few species are poisonous to man or beast. Indeed, many can be used as emergency rations, and foraging reindeer and caribou depend to an enormous extent on these lowly plants.

Dog Lichen

Peltigera canina

SIZE: 2½-8 in. long.

WHAT TO LOOK FOR: leathery sheet with scalloped edges; upper surface downy, blue-gray or pale brown (dry) to dark brown (moist); underside woolly, white to tan, with pale brown veins; fruiting bodies at edges, erect, rolled, resembling dog's teeth.

HABITAT: moist woods, shaded road banks.

Lung Lichen
Lobaria pulmonaria

SIZE: 2-10 in. wide.

WHAT TO LOOK FOR: irregularly lobed sheet with wrinkled surface; upper surface olive-brown (dry) to bright green (moist); underside mottled tan and white; loosely attached to tree.

HABITAT: on tree trunks; hardwood swamps, moist forests.

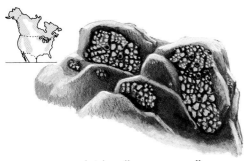

Map Lichen
Rhizocarpon geographicum

SIZE: ½-4 in. wide.

WHAT TO LOOK FOR: bright yellow to green-yellow crust with black outline and fine black cracks; fruiting bodies tiny, black, sunken in upper surface.

HABITAT: on exposed rocks; uplands, mountains.

Orange Star Lichen
Xanthoria elegans

SIZE:
1-2 in. wide.

WHAT TO LOOK FOR:
bright orange rosette; fruiting bodies saucer-shaped, abundant, in center; closely attached to rock.

HABITAT:
on exposed rocks, especially where birds perch; often on tombstones, lakeside boulders, and mountain cliffs.

Rock Tripe

(Toadskin Lichen)

Umbilicaria papulosa

SIZE:
1-4 in. wide.

WHAT TO LOOK FOR:
flat sheet with torn edges; blistered, light brown, brittle (dry) or leathery (moist) surface; fruiting bodies round, smooth, black; attached to rock by holdfast in center.

HABITAT:
exposed cliffs, ledges, boulders.

Cracked Shield Lichen

Parmelia sulcata

SIZE:
1-4 in. wide.

WHAT TO LOOK FOR:
flat leaflike plant with network of cracks and ridges; green-gray above, black below, with many short rootlike attachments.

HABITAT:
on tree trunks; woods, roadsides.

Beard Lichen

Usnea cavernosa

SIZE:
6-10 in. long.

WHAT TO LOOK FOR:
hanging tufts; pale green-gray, yellow-tinged threads attached to tree by central stem; stem often cracked, with white rubbery core exposed; branches vary in length.

HABITAT:
on trunks and limbs of conifers.

Reindeer Lichen

(Reindeer Moss)

Cladina rangiferina

SIZE:
2½-4 in. tall.

WHAT TO LOOK FOR:
large round gray clump; stems branched like antlers, with woolly surface and fingerlike tips; branches often perforated at base.

HABITAT:
on barren tundra soil; elsewhere in North, on sandy soil.

Ladder Lichen

Cladonia verticillata

SIZE:
1-3 in. tall.

WHAT TO LOOK FOR:
tiers of gray-green goblet-shaped cups (each rising from center of one below); flat scales at base, disappearing with age.

HABITAT:
in sandy soil and on old wood; fields, roadsides; in sun.

Pyxie Cups

Cladonia pyxidata

SIZE:
½ in. tall.

WHAT TO LOOK FOR:
gray stalked goblets, scaly inside and out; large lumpy scales around base of upright portion.

HABITAT:
in sand, on old wood, on soil-covered rocks; dry, sunny places.

British Soldiers

Cladonia cristatella

SIZE:
1-1½ in. tall.

WHAT TO LOOK FOR:
scarlet tips; stalks lumpy, scaly, gray (dry) or green-gray (moist); inconspicuous scales around base of upright portion.

HABITAT:
in sandy soil, on old wood; dry, sunny places.

Flabby Lichen

Evernia mesomorpha

<small>SIZE:</small>
2-4 in. long.

<small>WHAT TO LOOK FOR:</small>
drooping tufts; flabby, pale yellow-green, irregularly
angled branches; greenish powder on surface; attached to
tree at single point.

<small>HABITAT:</small>
on trunks of conifers; occasionally on broad-leaved trees.

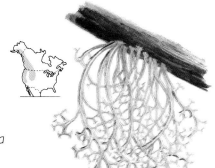

Wolf Lichen

Letharia vulpina

<small>SIZE:</small>
1-4 in. long.

<small>WHAT TO LOOK FOR:</small>
hanging tufts; irregular yellow to chartreuse branches;
powdery surface.

<small>HABITAT:</small>
on trunks and branches of conifers.

MUSHROOMS

The mushroom world is full of surprises. There are green mushrooms, purple ones, and others shaped like birds' nests complete with eggs. Some "blush" when bruised, some glow in the dark, and still others actually shoot up before your very eyes.

Mushrooms form part of the enormous group of organisms called fungi—organisms defined by their patterns of growth and their inability to make their own food. Like mosses and ferns, fungi reproduce by tiny spores rather than by flowers and seeds. In many species, such as the amanitas, spores develop only on the underside of the cap. In other species they are produced all over the surface (certain coral fungi) or on the inside (the puffballs).

Once released, the spores are dispersed from the parent plant. (The word "plant" is used loosely here, for many scientists put fungi into a separate kingdom.) Air currents blow them away; raindrops wash them away; flying insects transport them to distant places. When the spores land in a favorable location (say, moist soil), an underground network of threads, called a mycelium, develops. The mycelium is often white, and frequently you can find it by poking about in the soil, wood, or other material in which a mushroom or other fungus is growing.

The mycelium produces swellings that enlarge and eventually push above the surface, forming the fleshy structure—the mushroom—that produces spores. A few species, such as the highly prized truffles, never grow above the surface; they are strictly subterranean.

Although the mushroom itself (the part above ground) is generally short-lived, the mycelium may live for decades, even centuries. Its longevity depends on the food supply, for unlike green plants, fungi lack chlorophyll and are unable to make their own food. Where they get their food varies from species to species. Some, such as the Oyster Mushroom, use decaying wood or other dead plant material. Others nourish themselves on living plants (sometimes even other mushrooms) or animals, causing disease or death. One such species pictured in this book is the Orange-colored Cordyceps, which grows on insects.

Still other species—a great many, scientists have discovered—obtain their food from living trees in a way that benefits them both. The mycelium of the mushroom intertwines and fuses with the rootlets of the tree; the mushroom gets the food it needs, and the tree gets its essential nutrients. Sometimes the relationship between mushroom and tree is extraordinarily specific: a particular kind of mushroom will grow under or near only one kind of tree. So if you're "up" on tree identification, you'll have a head start on identifying mushrooms.

Mushroom hunting is an activity for all seasons, and there are even a few species, such as the Winter Mushroom, that "sprout" only when the

---

A Warning Against Eating Wild Mushrooms

Exploring for mushrooms, identifying them, and learning about how they live and grow give a great deal of pleasure to many people, but others are attracted to mushrooms because they are free and exotic food items. Eating wild mushrooms is extremely risky. Fatally poisonous species as well as ones that will make you unpleasantly ill grow throughout North America, and no general rule allows discrimination between those that are edible and those that are inedible or much worse. No wild mushroom should be eaten in any amount or in any form unless it has been identified by an expert and declared safe for eating.

Jack-o'-lantern

Chanterelle

One danger in eating wild mushrooms is that poisonous species can be confused with edible ones. Although the Chanterelle is often considered a "safe" species, it resembles the poisonous Jack-o'-lantern in shape, overall color, and spore color. While the differences may seem obvious, it is rare to have them both at hand for comparison.

weather is cold. But fall, especially after rain, is a prime time for finding mushrooms; wet springs are second-best. Like the famed swallows of Capistrano, mushrooms of a given species will often "return" to the same place at about the same time of year—though in reality, of course, they are there all along, their threads waiting beneath the surface.

HOW TO USE THIS SECTION

Different kinds of mushrooms are grouped together according to the location and nature of the structures that bear their spores.

Gilled mushroom

• The most prominent group, the gilled mushrooms and the closely related chanterelles, are shown on pages 202 through 239.

• The tube mushrooms, whose spongy undersides are perforated with small spore-producing openings, are shown on pages 243 through 246.

Tube mushroom

• The pore (or bracket) fungi, which are hard or firm and often grow like shelves on a stump or tree, have pores that open on the underside and produce the spores. This group begins at the top of page 247.

Pore fungus

• The teeth fungi, shown on pages 252 through 253, produce spores on hanging "teeth." The teeth may be on the underside only, or they may be all over the surface.

• Puffballs and their relatives, which open up to release their spores (the spores develop on the inside), are shown on pages 256 through 258.

Teeth fungus

• Other groups of fungi illustrated in this book are the following: the coral fungi (pages 240-242), the jelly fungi (pages 259-260), the flask fungi (pages 261-263), and the cup fungi (pages 263–269).

Puffball

Overall color. To identify mushrooms shown in this section, don't rely only on the color of the illustration; read the description too. Often a given species will occur in a variety of hues; location is important (mushrooms growing in sunshine tend to be paler than their shaded cousins), and so is age (an old Vermilion Hygrophorus will be yellow rather than vermilion). Of greater significance than color alone in identifying a mushroom is whether it shows stains (streaks or blotches of a different color) and whether the specimen changes color when bruised (slice a mushroom lengthwise and give it a pinch).

Spore color. Although single spores are invisible to the naked eye, spores en masse have a color, and that color is important in the identification of gilled mushrooms. To collect enough spores to observe their color, place the cap of the mushroom, rounded end up, on some white paper. Cover it with a bowl or drinking glass. Within a few hours, a dusting of spores should appear on the paper beneath the cap. If you don't see any, rub your finger along the paper; white spores will show up against your skin.

Attachment of gills. If the underside of the mushroom has thin plates, or gills, cut it lengthwise to see how the gills are connected with the stem. They may be free (that is, not attached to the stem), or they may be attached in one of several ways, as shown below.

gills not
attached to
stem

gills attached
to stem and
running down
stem

gills attached
to stem and
notched

gills attached
directly to stem

Amanitas *Amanitaceae*

The first sign of an amanita is the button, the egg-shaped young mushroom that in these species has a skin called the veil surrounding all parts. (In the button stage amanitas can be mistaken for puffballs.) As the parts expand, the veil bursts, leaving a telltale cup around the base of the stem or flecks or warts on the cap. Each year accidental poisonings and deaths result from eating poisonous amanitas because people confuse them with edible species or wrongly believe there is a way to rid them of their poisons.

Destroying Angel
Amanita virosa

<small>SIZE:</small>
1½-5 in. wide; stem 2-10 in. tall.

<small>WHAT TO LOOK FOR:</small>
cap usually smooth; gills free; stem with collar near top, bulbous base, and cup; all parts white.

<small>HABITAT:</small>
woods or under single tree.

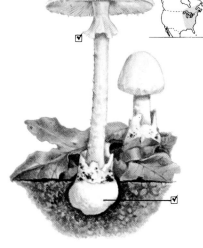

Death Cup
Amanita phalloides

<small>SIZE:</small>
2-6 in. wide; stem 2-6 in. tall.

<small>WHAT TO LOOK FOR:</small>
cap usually smooth, greenish yellow, green, olive, gray, or yellow-brown (may fade to pale yellow); gills free, white; stem white, with whitish or yellow collar near top, bulbous base, and whitish or yellow cup.

<small>HABITAT:</small>
all kinds of woods, especially under oaks or conifers; under single tree.

Fly Agaric
Amanita múscaria

SIZE:
2-7 in. wide; stem 3-7 in. tall.

WHAT TO LOOK FOR:
cap yellow, orange, orange-red, or dark red
(rarely white), with white warts unless
rain-washed; gills free, white to yellow;
stem white, with white to yellow collar at
top or middle and bulbous base with white
or yellow rings or scales.

HABITAT:
woods or under single tree.

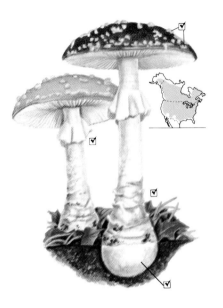

Panther Amanita
Amanita pantherina

SIZE:
2-5 in. wide; stem 2½-4 in. tall.

WHAT TO LOOK FOR:
cap brown, yellow-brown, or dingy yellow,
with whitish warts unless rain-washed; gills
free, white; stem white, with yellow or gray
collar near top or middle and club-shaped
base with rings, scales, or roll.

HABITAT:
usually under conifers.

Caesar's Mushroom

Amanita caesarea

SIZE:
2-6 in. wide; stem 3-6 in. tall.

WHAT TO LOOK FOR:
cap smooth, bright orange to red; gills free, yellow; stem orange-yellow, with orange-yellow collar near top and white cup.

HABITAT:
open woods; under conifers or oaks.

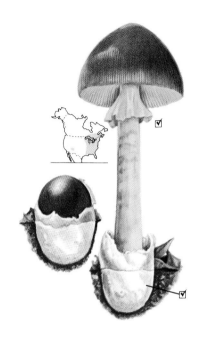

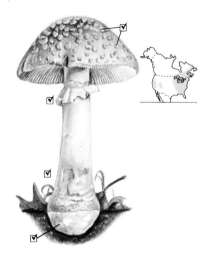

Blusher

Amanita rubescens

SIZE:
2-6 in. wide; stem 3-8 in. tall.

WHAT TO LOOK FOR:
cap whitish, buff, gray, or brown (develops a pink tinge), with white or gray warts unless rain-washed; gills almost free, white; stem whitish, with collar on top half and club-shaped to bulbous base, often with a few patches; all parts bruise red.

HABITAT:
open woods; under broad-leaved trees.

Napkin Amanita

Amanita citrina

SIZE:
1-5 in. wide; stem 2½-5 in. tall.

WHAT TO LOOK FOR:
cap pale greenish yellow, smooth or with flat
patches of gray or gray-pink; gills free, whitish
or yellow; stem white, with white or yellow
collar near top, soft bulbous base, and often
with an ill-defined cup.

HABITAT:
under broad-leaved trees or in mixed woods.

Grisette

Amanita vaginata

SIZE:
1½-3 in. wide; stem 3-5 in. tall.

WHAT TO LOOK FOR:
cap smooth, smoky gray; gills free,
white; stem whitish or gray, sometimes
with rings of flat hairs; no collar;
slightly bulbous base with white cup.

HABITAT:
all kinds of woods.

Lepiotas *Lepiotaceae*

Like many amanitas, lepiotas often have a collar on the stem; however, they never have a cup at the stem's base. A number of them thrive under man-made conditions. The Yellow Lepiota (*Lepiota lutea*) grows in greenhouses and in the soil of potted plants. The Blushing Lepiota (*Lepiota americana*), which "blushes" red when it is bruised, prefers the stumps of street and lawn trees, particularly maples.

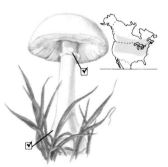

Parasol Mushroom

Lepiota procera

SIZE:
2½-6 in. wide; stem 6-10 in. tall.

WHAT TO LOOK FOR:
cap surface broken into red-brown scales (except in center), with whitish to pale tan between scales; gills free, white (pink, then brown, with age); stem whitish, with brown scales, movable fringed collar near top, and no cup; spores white.

HABITAT:
fields, lawns, woodland openings.

Smooth Lepiota

Leucoagaricus naucinus

SIZE:
1½-4 in. wide; stem 2½-5 in. tall.

WHAT TO LOOK FOR:
cap smooth, white (may be gray near center); gills free, white (grayish pink with age); stem white, with collar near top, club-shaped base, and no cup; cap and stem bruise slowly yellow; spores white to creamy.

HABITAT:
grassy areas.

Green Gill Mushroom

Chlorophyllum molybdites

SIZE:
3-12 in. wide; stem 3-10 in. tall.

WHAT TO LOOK FOR:
cap white to buff, with buff to brown scales; gills free, whitish (yellowish, then olive, with age); stem smooth, white (dingy brown when old or bruised), with movable collar near top and no cup; spores dull green; often grows in rings.

HABITAT:
grassy areas.

Shaggy Lepiota

Lepiota rachodes

SIZE:
3-8 in. wide; stem 4-8 in. tall.

WHAT TO LOOK FOR:
cap surface broken into pink-gray to dark brown scales, with whitish between scales; gills free, white (brown blotches with age); stem white (bruises yellow or red-brown), with fringed collar and no cup; spores white.

HABITAT:
woodlands, grassy areas, compost heaps, wood-chip mulch, woodsheds, greenhouses.

Hygrophori *Hygrophoraceae*

Red, orange, yellow, or shining white—these mushrooms' eye-catching colors add a glimmer of brightness to dimly lighted woods. The Parrot Hygrophorus (*Hygrophorus psittacinus*), widely distributed in North America, is a rich dark green, a most unusual color for a mushroom. One characteristic of this family is tactile: the gills feel waxy when rubbed hard between the fingers.

Cone-shaped Hygrophorus
Hygrophorus conicus

SIZE:
1-2½ in. wide; stem 2-4 in. tall.

WHAT TO LOOK FOR:
cap red to yellow-orange, often with olive tints; gills free or partially attached, white (olive, orange, or yellow with age); stem often colored like cap; all parts black when old or bruised; spores white.

HABITAT:
under conifers.

Vermilion Hygrophorus

Hygrophorus miniatus

SIZE:
½-1½ in. wide; stem 1-2 in. tall.

WHAT TO LOOK FOR:
cap red (fading to orange or yellow); gills
fully or partially attached; gills and stem
same color as cap or paler; spores white.

HABITAT:
in soil or moss under broad-leaved trees or
in mixed woods.

Russula Hygrophorus

Hygrophorus russula

SIZE:
2-4½ in. wide; stem 1-3 in. tall.

WHAT TO LOOK FOR:
cap slimy when wet, pink or pink-brown, often with
dark red streaks; gills attached or running down stem,
white (turning pink with dark red spots); stem white
(turning pink or red-brown); spores white.

HABITAT:
under oaks or in oak-pine woods.

Russulas and Lactarii *Russulaceae*

Named from the Latin *lactare* ("to secrete milk"), the lactarii ooze a milklike liquid when cut or broken. The milk can be white, carrot-orange, deep blood-red, or even blue, as in the southeastern Blue Lactarius (*Lactarius indigo*). The russulas (from the Latin for "reddish") lack milk and do not always come in the color their name suggests: they can be purple, yellow, orange, green, or even black. Both groups are common woodland mushrooms in summer and fall. Sometimes their caps are scored with teeth marks—a sign that a small mammal has come and gone.

Cottony-margined Milky Cap
Lactarius deceptivus

Size:
2-9 in. wide; stem 1½-4 in. tall.

What to look for:
young cap with cottony, rolled-under edge; gills running down stem; stem velvety; all parts white (tan or brown with age); milk white, slowly stains tissue brown; spores white.

Habitat:
under conifers, especially hemlocks, or in mixed woods.

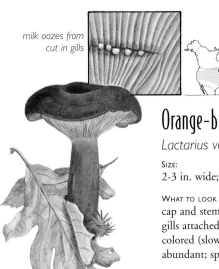

milk oozes from cut in gills

Orange-brown Lactarius

Lactarius volemus

SIZE:
2-3 in. wide; stem 2-3 in. tall.

WHAT TO LOOK FOR:
cap and stem brown to orange-buff, malodorous; gills attached or partially running down stem, cream colored (slowly bruise brown); milk white, sticky, abundant; spores white.

HABITAT:
under broad-leaved trees or in mixed woods.

Delicious Lactarius

Lactarius deliciosus

SIZE:
1½-4 in. wide; stem 1-2½ in. tall.

WHAT TO LOOK FOR:
cap, gills, and stem orange (dull green when old or bruised); cap and stem often with light spots; cap slimy or sticky when wet; gills running down stem; milk orange, not abundant.

HABITAT:
under conifers.

Pungent Russula

Russula emetica

2-4½ in. wide; stem 2-4½ in. tall.

WHAT TO LOOK FOR:
cap slimy, bright red (fades with age), with ridges on edge; gills attached, white; stem white; spores white.

HABITAT:
bogs; under conifers in moss.

Short-stemmed Russula

Russula brevipes

SIZE:
3-8 in. wide; stem 1-2 in. tall.

WHAT TO LOOK FOR:
cap depressed in center, white to pale buff (brown with age); gills partially running down stem, white or tinged green, often with brown spots; stem white (bruises brown).

HABITAT:
under conifers.

Tricholomas and Relatives *Tricholomataceae*

A large and diverse family of 1,000 or more species, these mushrooms have little in common except white or lightly colored spores. All of the species on pages 213 to 224, except for the Split-gilled Mushroom, belong to this group. Some grow on wood, others in soil, but like all mushrooms, they spring from rootlike filaments called mycelia. The mycelium of the Honey Mushroom can spread underground from the roots of one living tree to another and, unlike most mushrooms, can kill its host. This mycelium is luminescent, causing a glow known as fox fire. The mycelium of the Fairy Ring spreads under lawns in ever-expanding circles, creating dark green rings as it stimulates the growth of grass.

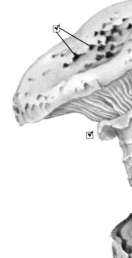

Scaly Lentinus
Lentinus lepideus

SIZE:
2-8 in. wide; stem 1½-6 in. tall.

WHAT TO LOOK FOR:
cap whitish to buff, developing small brown scales; gills running down stem, rather far apart, toothed at edges, whitish to buff; stem whitish, with collar near top (often scaly below collar); with age stem turns yellow, base brown to wine-red; spores white to buff.

HABITAT:
on conifer wood.

Split-gilled Mushroom
Schizophyllum commune

SIZE:
½-1 in. wide.

WHAT TO LOOK FOR:
cap hairy, tough, fan-shaped, white to gray (brownish gray when wet); gills gray, radiating from point of attachment, with edges split or grooved; no stem; spores pinkish.

HABITAT:
usually in clusters on logs, sticks, stumps of broad-leaved trees.

Maroon Tricholoma
Tricholomopsis rutilans

SIZE:
1½-4 in. wide; stem 2-4 in. tall.

WHAT TO LOOK FOR:
cap dry, reddish, with hairs or fine scales; gills fully or partially attached, yellow; stem yellow beneath purple-red hairs (bruises darker yellow); fragrant odor; spores white.

HABITAT:
on conifer logs and stumps.

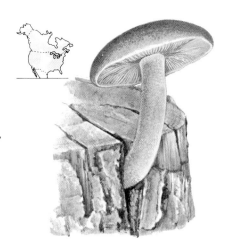

Golden Trumpets

Xeromphalina campanella

SIZE:
½-1 in. wide; stem ½-1½ in. tall.

WHAT TO LOOK FOR:
cap orange-yellow or yellow-brown to orange-brown, with stripes on edge; gills running down stem, somewhat far apart, yellow to orange; stem yellow at top, red-brown at base; hairs on base; spores buff.

HABITAT:
in clusters on conifer logs and stumps.

Club-footed Clitocybe

Clitocybe clavipes

SIZE:
1-4 in. wide; stem 1½-3 in. tall.

WHAT TO LOOK FOR:
cap brown or gray-brown, often with paler margin; gills running down stem, white to cream; stem brown or dingy buff, with bulbous base; spores white.

HABITAT:
under conifers; sometimes in mixed woods.

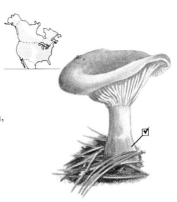

Oyster Mushroom

Pleurotus ostreatus

SIZE:
1½-12 in. wide.

WHAT TO LOOK FOR:
cap fan- or shell-shaped, gray or brown-gray (white with age); gills white, radiating from point of attachment; if present, stem white, off-center or at rear of cap; spores grayish lilac.

HABITAT:
in overlapping clusters on logs and stumps of broad-leaved trees.

Parasitic Asterophora

Asterophora lycoperdoides

SIZE:
½-1 in. wide; stem about 1 in. tall.

WHAT TO LOOK FOR:
cap smooth and whitish (powdery and brown when mature); gills attached, whitish, far apart, sometimes narrow and nearly invisible; stem whitish (brown with age); spores brown.

HABITAT:
on rotting mushrooms, especially russulas and lactarii.

Little Wheel Mushroom

Marasmius rotula

SIZE:
¼-¾ in. wide; stem ½-3 in. tall.

WHAT TO LOOK FOR:
cap white, with dark center and ribbed edge; gills white, far apart, joined to collar neat top of stem; stem mostly black, shiny, wirelike; spores white.

HABITAT:
in clusters on decaying leaves or wood under broad-leaved trees.

Honey Mushroom

Armillariella mellea

SIZE:
1-5 in. wide; stem 1½-6 in. tall.

WHAT TO LOOK FOR:
cap slimy when wet, and light to dark yellow, honey-colored, or brown, with fine hairs or scales over center; gills attached or running down stem, white or cream (spotted brown with age); stem white to buff or brown, with collar near top; black stringlike growths in nearby wood and soil; spores white or pale cream.

HABITAT:
in clusters on logs and stumps; sometimes at base of tree.

Wood Blewit
Clitocybe nuda

SIZE:
1½-6 in. wide; stem 1¼-4 in. tall.

WHAT TO LOOK FOR:
cap violet (fading to violet-gray or buff, then brown); gills partially attached, pale violet (buff to brown with age); stem pale violet (base turning brown), often with fine white hairs; spores flesh color.

HABITAT:
woods; occasionally in compost piles.

Pine Mushroom
Armillaria ponderosa

SIZE:
2½-8 in. wide; stem 1¾-7 in. tall.

WHAT TO LOOK FOR:
cap white when young (center turning brown and scaly, edge becoming streaked with flat brown hairs); gills partially attached, white (bruise brown); rufflelike collar; stem white above collar, red-brown and scaly or hairy below; spores white.

HABITAT:
under conifers.

Bleeding Mycena

Mycena haematopus

SIZE:
½-1½ in. wide; stem 1-3 in. tall.

WHAT TO LOOK FOR:
cap conical to bell-shaped (often with fringed edge), red-brown in center, red-gray at edge; gills white or gray-red (spotted red-brown with age); stem brown (bleeds red when cut); spores white.

HABITAT:
on decaying logs.

Clean Mycena

Mycena pura

SIZE:
½-1½ in. wide; stem 1-4 in. tall.

WHAT TO LOOK FOR:
cap lilac, purple, or dull rose (sometimes tinted gray or brown), with radishlike odor; gills fully or partially attached, white (turning color of cap with age); stem white or color of cap; spores white.

HABITAT: woods.

Golden Mycena

Mycena leaiana

SIZE:
½-1½ in. wide; stem ¾-3½ in. tall.

WHAT TO LOOK FOR:
cap shiny, slimy, bright orange (orange-yellow with age); gills attached, salmon-orange or orange-yellow, with bright red-orange edges; stem slimy, orange to yellow; spores white.

HABITAT:
in clusters on logs and stumps of broad-leaved trees.

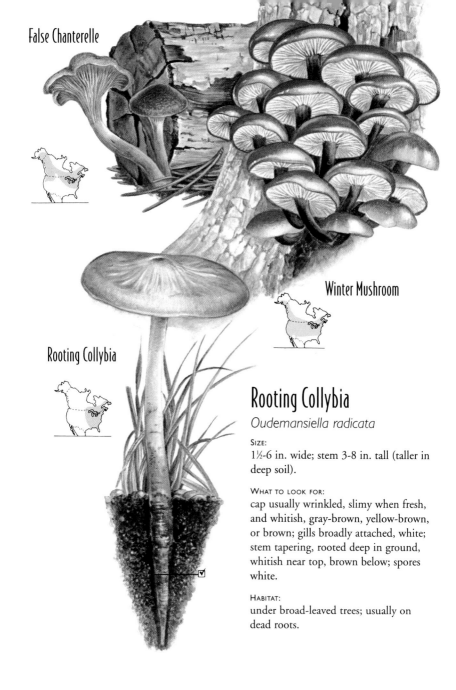

False Chanterelle

Winter Mushroom

Rooting Collybia

Rooting Collybia

Oudemansiella radicata

SIZE:
1½-6 in. wide; stem 3-8 in. tall (taller in deep soil).

WHAT TO LOOK FOR:
cap usually wrinkled, slimy when fresh, and whitish, gray-brown, yellow-brown, or brown; gills broadly attached, white; stem tapering, rooted deep in ground, whitish near top, brown below; spores white.

HABITAT:
under broad-leaved trees; usually on dead roots.

◄False Chanterelle

Hygrophoropsis aurantiaca

SIZE:
¾-3 in. wide; stem ¾-2½ in. tall.

WHAT TO LOOK FOR:
cap dark orange-brown or brown when young, bright orange when mature, often with dark center; gills regularly forked, running down stem, bright orange; stem pale to dark orange; spores white to cream.

HABITAT:
usually on or near logs and stumps under conifers.

◄Winter Mushroom

Flammulina velutipes

SIZE:
1-3 in. wide; stem 1-4 in. tall.

WHAT TO LOOK FOR:
cap slimy, brown-orange or brown-yellow; gills running down stem and notched, white (buff with age); stem velvety, white (turning yellow at top, dark brown below); spores white.

HABITAT:
in clusters on logs and stumps of broad-leaved trees.

Jack-o'-lantern

Omphalotus olearius

SIZE:
2-5 in wide; stem 2-8 in. tall.

WHAT TO LOOK FOR:
cap, gills, and stem orange to orange-yellow, malodorous; gills running down stem, luminescent in the dark; spores white or cream.

HABITAT:
in large clusters on stumps, buried roots (often of oaks).

Greenish-yellow Tricholoma

Tricholoma flavovirens

SIZE:
2-5 in. wide; stem 1-4 in. tall.

WHAT TO LOOK FOR:
cap green-yellow, with center often brown; gills partially attached, yellow; stem yellow-tinged, white at top; spores white.

HABITAT:
woods; especially under pines, hemlocks, or aspens.

Dingy Tricholoma

Tricholoma portentosum

SIZE:
1½-4 in wide; stem 2-5 in. tall.

WHAT TO LOOK FOR:
cap with flattened fine dark hairs, gray or gray-brown, sometimes violet-tinted; gills attached or notched, pale yellow; stem white or yellowish; spores white.

HABITAT:
under conifers.

Waxy Laccaria

Laccaria laccata

SIZE:
½-2 in. wide; stem 1-4 in. tall.

WHAT TO LOOK FOR:
cap smooth to rough and brown, pink-brown, or dull flesh color (paler with age); gills attached or partially running down stem, somewhat far apart, pink; stem colored like cap; spores white.

HABITAT:
on moss, humus, or wet soil in woods; sometimes in open areas.

Russet-scaly Tricholoma

Tricholoma vaccinum

SIZE:
1½-3 in. wide; stem 2-3 in. tall.

WHAT TO LOOK FOR:
cap with fine flat hairs or scales (woolly edge when young), dry, red-brown; gills attached or notched, white, with red-brown streaks or spots; stem with fine flat hairs, red-brown; spores white.

HABITAT:
under conifers.

Fairy Ring

Marasmius oreades

SIZE:
¾-2 in. wide; stem 1-3 in. tall.

WHAT TO LOOK FOR:
cap often humped in center, light tan, cream, brown, or red-brown; gills partially attached or free, white to pale buff; stem white to buff at top, buff to brown and often hairy at base; spores white to buff.

HABITAT:
in groups, arcs, or rings in grassy areas.

Volvarias *Pluteaceae*

Most of the mushrooms in this book are encountered fairly frequently. The Silky Volvaria is an exception. It is rare, as are the half dozen or so other native volvarias, and its striking beauty makes it a choice find. All the members of this small family have dull pink or rose spores. (The only other mushrooms with pink spores are the rhodophylls and some tricholomas.) The cup at the base of the stem further distinguishes some volvarias, but this feature is lacking in the plutei, the more common group in the family.

Silky Volvaria

Volvariella bombycina

SIZE:
2-8 in. wide; stem 2-8 in. tall.

WHAT TO LOOK FOR:
cap silky, often with fringed edge, white (slightly yellow with age); gills free, white (pink, then dull rose, with age); stem often curved, white, with deep cup at base, no ring; spores dull pink, rose, or brown-pink.

HABITAT:
on logs and stumps of broad-leaved trees and wounds in living trees.

Rhodophylls *Entolomataceae*

Although the mushrooms in this group are difficult to tell apart, they are easily distinguished from other families. The rhodophylls ("rosy-leaved") have at least one characteristic—rose-colored spores—in common with the volvarias, but their gills are attached to the top of the stem and they have no cup at the base. The fleshy white masses that immediately identify the Abortive Entoloma are malformations; the mycelium of the Honey Mushroom has penetrated the entoloma and caused the entoloma to become deformed.

Livid Entoloma

Entoloma sinuatum

SIZE:
2½-6 in. wide; stem 1½-6 in. tall.

WHAT TO LOOK FOR:
cap pale dingy tan or gray-tan; gills notched at stem, whitish to yellow (dingy pink with age); stem thick, solid, white; spores dingy pink.

HABITAT:
in mixed woods or under conifers.

Salmon Entoloma

Entoloma salmoneum

SIZE:
¾-2 in. wide; stem 1½-4½ in. tall.

WHAT TO LOOK FOR:
cap conical to bell-shaped, salmon-colored; gills fully or partially attached, orange-salmon; stem colored like cap; spores brown-pink.

HABITAT:
woods, bogs.

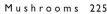

Abortive Entoloma

Entoloma abortivum

SIZE:
1½-4 in. wide; stem 1½-4 in. tall.

WHAT TO LOOK FOR:
cap gray or brown-gray, sometimes with watery spots; gills attached or running down stem, gray (dingy rose with age); stem gray-white; fleshy white masses often appear nearby.

HABITAT:
on decaying wood and humus.

malformed (aborted) entoloma

Gomphidii *Gomphidiaceae*

The Greek word *gomphos* means "nail" or "peg," a possible allusion to the shape of young mushrooms belonging to this group. When mature, the gills are dark brown or black; they are thick, extend far down the stem, and look somewhat waxy. All 25 species grow under conifers.

Slimy Gomphidius

Gomphidius glutinosus

SIZE:
1-4 in. wide; stem 1½-4 in. tall.

WHAT TO LOOK FOR:
cap slimy and gray-brown, red-brown, or purple-gray (blotched black with age); gills running down stem, white (gray with age); stem yellow below slimy collar, white above; spores gray to black.

HABITAT:
under conifers.

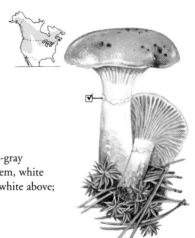

Stropharias and Relatives *Strophariaceae*

Many, but not all, of the hallucinogenic mushrooms belong to this colorful family. Certain of the small, rare psilocybes have long been used by Mexican Indians in religious ceremonies; possession of the Cuban Psilocybe (*Psilocybe cubensis*), which grows in Florida and along the Gulf Coast, is illegal in most states.

Brick Top

Naematoloma sublateritium

SIZE:
¾-4 in. wide; stem 2-4 in. tall.

WHAT TO LOOK FOR:
cap brick-red at center, buff and often fringed with hairs (at edge); gills attached, dingy white (purple-gray with age); stem white, often with thin hairy collar near top; spores purple-brown.

HABITAT:
in clusters on logs and stumps of broad-leaved trees.

Smoky-gilled Woodlover

Naematoloma capnoides

SIZE:
¾-3 in. wide; stem 2-4 in. tall.

WHAT TO LOOK FOR:
cap rounded (becoming flattened) and orange, rust, or
yellow-brown, with yellow edge; gills attached (becoming free),
white (gray, then purple-brown, with age); stem yellow on top with
slight hairy ring, brown to rusty below; spores purple-brown.

HABITAT:
in clusters on or near conifer wood.

Sulphur Top

Naematoloma fasciculare

SIZE:
½-3 in. wide; stem 2-5 in. tall.

WHAT TO LOOK FOR:
cap green-yellow or yellow (center
may be orange or brown); gills attached (becoming free), sulphur- or
green-yellow; stem white at top with slight hairy ring, brown below;
spores purple-brown.

HABITAT:
in clusters on logs and stumps of conifers or broad-leaved trees.

Inky Caps and Relatives *Coprinaceae*

The caps and gills of the fungi in this family—many of them known as inky caps—blacken with age and melt into an inklike liquid. As the spore-containing liquid drips to the ground, the species renews itself. Fresh Shaggy Manes and some other inky caps are eaten, but once they have started to melt, they should be left alone. Some species are poisonous, and at least one, the Inky Cap, causes nausea if consumed with alcohol.

Inky Cap

Coprinus atramentarius

SIZE:
¾-3 in. wide; stem 1½-6 in. tall.

WHAT TO LOOK FOR:
cap conical to bell-shaped, light brown to gray (inky with age); gills white (gray, then black, with age); stem white, with flattened collar; spores black.

HABITAT:
on decaying logs, stumps, buried wood.

Haymaker's Mushroom

Psathyrella foenisecii

SIZE:
½-1½ in. wide; stem 1-3 in. tall.

WHAT TO LOOK FOR:
cap dark brown, red-brown, or gray-brown (pale tan with age); gills attached, brown or purple-brown; stem brittle, tan or dingy white; spores dark purple-brown.

HABITAT:
grassy areas.

Glistening Inky Cap
Coprinus micaceus

SIZE:
¾-2½ in. wide; stem 1-3 in. tall.

WHAT TO LOOK FOR:
cap conical to bell-shaped, brown or tan, with shiny grains when young (smooth, turning inky with age); gills white (turning inky); stem white; spores black.

HABITAT:
in clusters on decaying logs, stumps, buried wood.

MELTING
CAP

Shaggy Mane
Coprinus comatus

SIZE:
¾-2½ in. wide; stem 3-8 in. tall.

WHAT TO LOOK FOR:
cap columnar, white with brown top and scales (edges flaring out, cap turning inky, with age); gills white (pink, then inky, with age); stem white, with collar and bulbous base; spores black.

HABITAT:
lawns, pastures, roadsides.

Meadow Mushrooms and Relatives *Agaricaceae*

Although the mushrooms generally sold in stores are meadow mushrooms (they belong to a species native to Europe), wild meadow mushrooms—or any others, for that matter—should not be eaten unless their identity has been verified by an expert. Young mushrooms in this family are easy to confuse with the deadly amanitas.

Horse Mushroom

Agaricus arvensis

SIZE:
2½-8 in. wide; stem 2½-8 in. tall.

WHAT TO LOOK FOR:
cap white or cream (bruises yellow), sometimes with yellow center or fringed edge; gills free, white (gray-pink, then black-brown, with age); stem white (bruises yellow), with collar (has cottony patches on underside); spores brown.

HABITAT:
grassy areas.

Meadow Mushroom

Agaricus campestris

SIZE:
¾-4 in. wide; stem 1-3 in. tall.

WHAT TO LOOK FOR:
cap white or off-white, sometimes
with brown streaks or scales and
fringed edge; gills free, pink (purple-brown, then
black, with age); stem white, with thin collar near top
that soon disappears; spores dark purple-brown.

HABITAT:
open grassy areas.

Flat-topped Mushroom

Agaricus placomyces

SIZE:
1½-4 in. wide; stem 3-6 in. tall.

WHAT TO LOOK FOR:
cap white, with gray- or black-brown scales
(especially at center), malodorous; gills free,
white (pink, then purple-brown, with age);
stem with collar near top, whitish (turning
brown near base); spores brown.

HABITAT:
woods; usually under broad-leaved trees.

Paxilli *Paxillaceae*

The soft gills of the mushrooms in this small family (four or five species) separate cleanly from the underside of the cap when you press on them with a finger. The Black-footed Paxillus (*Paxillus atrotomentosus*), with rolled-under edge and hairy stem, is common under conifers.

Involute Paxillus

Paxillus involutus

SIZE:
1½-6 in wide; stem 1½-4 in. tall.

WHAT TO LOOK FOR:
cap light yellow-brown (brown or red-brown with age), with edge rolled under and ribbed until old; gills running down stem, yellow-olive (bruise brown); stem yellow-brown, often with brown streaks or blotches; spores brown.

HABITAT:
under conifers or in mixed woods.

Bolbitii and Relatives *Bolbitiaceae*

The Brownie Cap, a common inhabitant of lawns, is so fragile that it often lasts less than a day—a characteristic shared by many other species in this family. The name of the group comes from the Greek *bolbiton*, "cow dung," on which some of the species grow. The spores of all are brownish, ranging from rusty to earth tones.

Brownie Cap

Conocybe tenera

SIZE:
½-1 in. wide; stem 1½-3 in. tall.

WHAT TO LOOK FOR:
cap conical or bell-shaped, brown (tan with age); gills partially attached or free, brown; stem thin, fragile, brown; spores red-brown.

HABITAT:
grassy areas; sometimes in open woods.

Cortinarii and Relatives *Cortinariaceae*

A cobweblike veil called the cortina (Latin for "curtain") hangs from the edge of young cortinarius caps. As in all mushroom families, some species in this large, diverse group are poisonous—notably some galerinas, the only mushrooms besides the amanitas to contain amatoxins, deadly poisons that attack the liver and kidneys and have no known antidote. Other mushroom poisons produce severe reactions but are not usually fatal.

Scaly Pholiota

Pholiota squarrosoides

SIZE:
1-4 in. wide; stem 1½-4 in. tall.

WHAT TO LOOK FOR:
cap white to buff, slimy beneath pointed brown scales; gills attached or notched, white (brown with age); stem white with buff to brown scales, smooth at top, with hairy ring when young; spores brown.

HABITAT:
in clusters on logs and stumps of broad-leaved trees.

Clustered Inocybe
Inocybe fastigiata

SIZE:
¾-2 in. wide; stem 1½-3 in. tall.

WHAT TO LOOK FOR:
cap conical or bell-shaped (edge may be split), tan or yellow-brown, with flat radiating hairs, fishy-smelling; gills partially attached or notched, white (gray or olive, then brown, with age); stem white to brown; spores brown.

HABITAT:
woods.

Autumn Galerina
Galerina autumnalis

SIZE:
1-2½ in. wide; stem 1-3 in. tall.

WHAT TO LOOK FOR:
cap slimy, yellow-brown to brown; gills attached or running down stem, rusty brown; stem brown, with white streaks, thin collar when young; spores rusty brown.

HABITAT:
on logs.

Red-zoned Cortinarius
Cortinarius armillatus

SIZE:
2-5 in. wide; stem 2½-6 in. tall.

WHAT TO LOOK FOR:
cap red-brown; gills fully or partially attached, rusty brown; stem brown, with red bands; spores rusty brown.

HABITAT:
under birches or in mixed woods.

Cinnamon Cortinarius

Cortinarius cinnamomeus

SIZE:
1-2 in. wide; stem 1-3 in. tall.

WHAT TO LOOK FOR:
cap brown or yellow-brown; gills attached,
yellow (brown with age); stem yellow or
brown; spores rusty brown.

HABITAT:
under conifers.

Red-gilled Cortinarius

Cortinarius semisanguineus

SIZE:
¾-3 in. wide; stem 1-3 in. tall.

WHAT TO LOOK FOR:
gills dark blood-red, attached; cap brown-yellow;
stem dull yellow; spores rusty brown.

HABITAT:
in moss under conifers.

Violet Cortinarius

Cortinarius violaceus

SIZE:
2-4 in. wide; stem 2½-5 in. tall.

WHAT TO LOOK FOR:
cap, gills, and stem dark violet; gills
fully or partially attached; spores rusty
brown.

HABITAT:
conifer woods.

Chanterelles and Relatives *Cantharellaceae*

Frilly-edged and frequently trumpet-shaped, the top of a chanterelle looks like that of a typical mushroom. The underside, however, is different: the gills, if present, are widely spaced, have blunt edges, and are often forked or connected by ridges. These culinary delights of summer and early fall can, in some cases, unfortunately be confused with such inedible species as the Jack-o'-lantern and False Chanterelle.

Chanterelle

Cantharellus cibarius

SIZE:
¾-6 in. wide; stem 1-3 in. tall.

WHAT TO LOOK FOR:
cap yellow to orange; gills orange-buff, rather far apart, forked, blunt-edged; stem colored like cap or gills, or paler (bruises dark); spores whitish or pale buff.

HABITAT:
woods, roadsides.

Deceptive Craterellus

Craterellus fallax

SIZE:
1-3 in. wide; 1-5 in. tall.

WHAT TO LOOK FOR:
cap funnel-shaped, dark brown (blackish, then gray-brown, with age); underside smooth or slightly wrinkled (no gills), brown (bruises black; turns gray or yellow-gray with age); stem continuous with cap, hollow; spores orange-buff.

HABITAT:
woods.

Gill-less Chanterelle

Cantharellus lateritius

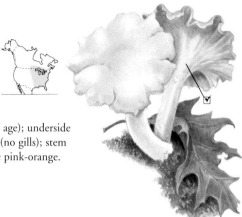

SIZE:
1-3½ in. wide; stem 1-2 in. tall.

WHAT TO LOOK FOR:
cap orange (pale yellow-orange with age); underside
pale buff, smooth or slightly ridged (no gills); stem
colored like cap or paler; spores pale pink-orange.

HABITAT:
open broad-leaved woods.

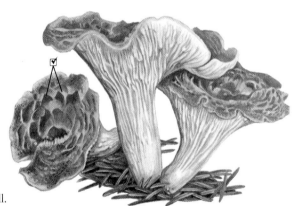

Shaggy Chanterelle

Gomphus floccosus

SIZE:
1½-6½ in. wide; 3½-8 in. tall.

WHAT TO LOOK FOR:
cap funnel-shaped, scaly, sometimes slimy, and yellow-orange,
orange, or red-orange (paler with age); gills in form of blunt, shallow
ridges and wrinkles; gills and stem cream; spores brown-yellow.

HABITAT:
coniferous or mixed woods.

Pig's Ears

Gomphus clavatus

SIZE:
1-4 in. wide; 2-5 in. tall.

WHAT TO LOOK FOR:
cap flat (depressed with age), pale purple (dingy pale yellow or buff with age); gills in form of shallow veins and ridges, often wrinkled, buff or purple (brownish with age); stem continuous with cap, dingy buff or pale lilac; spores orange-brown.

HABITAT:
coniferous woods.

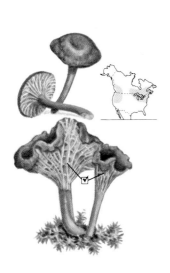

Tubed Cantharellus

Cantharellus tubaeformis

SIZE:
½-2½ in. wide; stem 1-2 in. tall.

WHAT TO LOOK FOR:
cap dark yellow-brown to brown (paler and gray with age); gills far apart, yellow (gray or violet with age), forked, blunt-edged; stem yellow to orange; spores white or yellow.

HABITAT:
wet woods, mossy logs.

Coral Fungi *Clavariaceae*

Most of these colorful, fleshy fungi are saprophytes, taking their nutrients from decaying material. A few species are believed to obtain nutrients from living trees, for their "roots" (mycelia) are connected with the roots of the trees. Coral fungi are gill-less, producing spores on the surface of their branches or, in unbranched species, on most of the outside surface.

Club Mushroom

Clavariadelphus truncatus

SIZE:
1-2½ in. wide at top; 3-6 in. tall.

WHAT TO LOOK FOR:
clublike shape; top flattened, wrinkled, yellow (gold, then pink-brown, with age); base white.

HABITAT:
under conifers.

Golden Clavaria

Ramaria aurea

SIZE:
clump 2-6 in. wide, 2-5 in. tall; stem 1-2 in. tall.

WHAT TO LOOK FOR:
branches golden, pale orange, or orange-buff, with yellow tips; stem white; does not change color when injured.

HABITAT:
under broad-leaved trees.

Gray Coral

Clavulina cinerea

SIZE:
clump ¾-2½ in. wide; 1-4 in. tall.

WHAT TO LOOK FOR:
many gray branches; base often white; branches become narrower toward top.

HABITAT:
in clumps on moss and needles under conifers.

Cauliflower Mushroom

Sparassis radicata

SIZE:
6-14 in. wide; 6-12 in. tall.

WHAT TO LOOK FOR:
cauliflowerlike shape; flattened, leaflike white to yellow "branches"; stem rooted below ground.

HABITAT:
under conifers.

Crowned Clavaria

Clavicorona pyxidata

SIZE:
clump 1-3½ in. wide; 2-4 in. tall.

WHAT TO LOOK FOR:
slender branches with crownlike tips, white or yellow (pale tan or pink-tan with age, finally brown on lower branches).

HABITAT:
in clumps on logs and stumps of broad-leaved trees.

Spindle Coral

Clavulinopsis fusiformis

SIZE:
⅛-½ in. wide; ½-6 in. tall.

WHAT TO LOOK FOR:
tall, thin, bright yellow spindle, often with pointed tip; large ones often flattened.

HABITAT:
in clusters in open woods.

Tube Mushrooms *Boletaceae and Strobilomycetaceae*

Instead of gills, tube mushrooms have tubes that open on the underside of the cap and give it a spongelike appearance. Some species retain remnants of the veil (the skin surrounding the young mushroom) as a collar or ring on the stem. The fungi in this group associate with trees; that is, the underground portion of the mushroom is connected with tree rootlets. The relationship may be so rigid that a particular species can grow only under one kind of tree.

Slippery Jack
Suillus luteus

SIZE:
1½-6 in wide; stem 1½-4 in. tall.

WHAT TO LOOK FOR:
cap slimy, brown, yellow-brown, or red-brown; underside white or yellow, with tube openings; stem dotted, pale yellow, with collar; spores dull red-brown.

HABITAT:
under pines or spruces.

Hollow-stemmed Boletinus
Suillus cavipes

SIZE:
1-4 in. wide; stem 1½-3½ in. tall.

WHAT TO LOOK FOR:
cap dry, hairy, and brown, red-brown, or orange-brown; underside yellow (dingy yellow with age), with tubes running down stem; stem hollow at bottom, with thin collar (soon flattening to slight ring), yellow above collar, brown below; spores brown.

HABITAT:
under larches.

Painted Bolete

Suillus pictus

SIZE:
1-4 in. wide; stem 1½-4 in. tall.

WHAT TO LOOK FOR:
cap with dull red scales and hairs (yellow flesh often showing between scales); underside yellow (bruises brown), with tube openings; stem with collar or ring, yellow above collar, white or red below; spores brown.

HABITAT:
under Eastern White Pine.

American Yellow Bolete

Suillus americanus

SIZE:
1-4 in. wide; stem 1-3½ in. tall.

WHAT TO LOOK FOR:
cap bright yellow, with patches of buff to brown (young with fringed edge); underside dull yellow (bruises brown), with tube openings; stem bright yellow, with red or red-brown dots; spores dull red-brown.

HABITAT:
under Eastern White Pine.

Greville's Bolete

Suillus grevillei

SIZE:
2-6 in. wide; stem 1½-4 in. tall.

WHAT TO LOOK FOR:
cap slimy, brown-red or yellow; underside yellow (bruises brown; turns olive-yellow with age), with tube openings; stem with collar, yellow above collar, streaked red-brown below; spores brown.

HABITAT:
under larches.

Two-colored Bolete

Boletus bicolor

SIZE:
2-6 in. wide; stem 2-4 in. tall.

WHAT TO LOOK FOR:
cap purple-red (paler with age, often cracking to show yellow); underside bright yellow (bruises blue), with tube openings; stem yellow near top, purple-red below; spores olive-green.

HABITAT:
under broad-leaved trees.

Old Man of the Woods

Strobilomyces floccopus

SIZE:
1½-6 in. wide; stem 2-6 in. tall.

WHAT TO LOOK FOR:
cap scaly or shaggy (young with fringed edge), gray to black; underside white (bruises red, then black; turns gray with age), with tube openings; stem shaggy; spores black.

HABITAT:
under broad-leaved trees.

Admirable Bolete

Boletus mirabilis

SIZE:
2-8 in. wide; stem 3-8 in. tall.

WHAT TO LOOK FOR:
cap dark red-brown, woolly or hairy when young; underside bright yellow, with tube openings; stem red-brown, with netlike ridges near top; spores brown.

HABITAT:
on or near conifer logs and stumps.

Bitter Bolete

Tylopilus felleus

SIZE:
2-12 in. wide; stem 1½-6 in. tall.

WHAT TO LOOK FOR:
cap tan to brown; underside white (bruises
brown; turns pink, then rose, with age), with
tube openings; stem white near top, brown
below, with netlike ridges; spores dull pink or
rose.

HABITAT:
near logs and stumps of conifers.

King Bolete

Boletus edulis

SIZE:
3-10 in. wide; stem 4-7 in. tall.

WHAT TO LOOK FOR:
cap pale brown to brown; underside white (green-
yellow with age), with tube openings; stem
bulbous, white near top, yellow to brown below,
with netlike ridges; spores brown.

HABITAT:
under conifers.

Pore Fungi *Polyporaceae and Ganodermataceae*

Sometimes called bracket fungi, the species on pages 247 through 251 form shelflike protuberances on trees, stumps, and logs. On the underside of the cap are pores similar in appearance and function (they produce spores) to the tubes of tube mushrooms. The pores vary greatly in size, some being visible only through a magnifying glass. In contrast to tube mushrooms, pore fungi are usually tough and woody, especially the older ones. When an Artist's Fungus is young, for example, its underside is soft enough to draw on with a sharp instrument, but it slowly dries and hardens, preserving the picture in the process. As pore fungi age, they grow, sometimes to a very large size. One specimen of the rare Noble Polypore (*Oxyporus nobilissimus*) growing on a spruce in the Pacific Northwest weighed an impressive 300 pounds.

Artist's Fungus

Ganoderma applanatum

SIZE:
2-20 in. wide.

WHAT TO LOOK FOR:
cap hard, woody, semicircular or fan-shaped, pale to dark gray or gray-brown, with ridges and furrows; underside white to pale brown (bruises dark brown); stem absent.

HABITAT:
on logs and stumps of broad-leaved trees; in wounds in living trees.

Many-colored Polypore

Coriolus versicolor

SIZE:
single cap ¾-3 in. wide.

WHAT TO LOOK FOR:
clusters of thin overlapping caps, with gray, blue, and black bands or white, yellow, and brown bands; velvety or hairy zones alternating with smooth zones; underside white or yellow; stem absent.

HABITAT:
on dead wood or in wounds in broad-leaved trees; occasionally on conifers.

Hemlock Polypore

Ganoderma tsugae

SIZE:
2-8 in. wide; stem (if present) 1-6 in. long.

WHAT TO LOOK FOR:
cap mahogany-red, fan-shaped, shiny or dusty brown; underside white or brown; stem mahogany-red, shiny, centered or attached at back.

HABITAT:
on or near conifer stumps and logs.

Hen of the Woods
Grifola frondosa

SIZE:
8-25 in. wide.

WHAT TO LOOK FOR:
large cluster of overlapping caps, gray on top, white or yellow below; stem short, thick, with many branches.

HABITAT:
near stumps or trunks, usually of broad-leaved trees.

Sulphur Polypore
Polyporus sulphureus

SIZE:
2-20 in. wide.

WHAT TO LOOK FOR:
cap fleshy or firm, with ruffled edge; orange, salmon, or yellow (paler with age) above; underside sulphur yellow (paler with age); stem short or absent.

HABITAT:
in large clusters on trunks, logs, and stumps of conifers and broad-leaved trees.

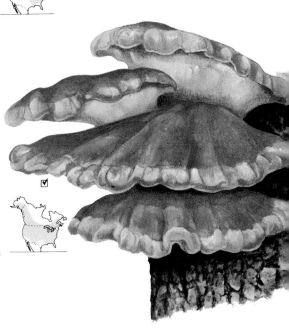

Red Belt Fungus
Fomitopsis pinicola

SIZE:
2-16 in. wide.

WHAT TO LOOK FOR:
cap hard or woody, thick, dark red to brown or gray to black, sticky, with red band near rounded edge; underside white to yellow (brown with age).

HABITAT:
on dead trees, stumps, or logs; occasionally on living trees.

Bracket Fomes
Fomes fomentarius

SIZE:
2-8 in. wide.

WHAT TO LOOK FOR:
cap hoof-shaped, tough, with hard crust, pale tan to gray-brown (gray to black with age); underside gray to brown; stem absent.

HABITAT:
on dead trunks or logs of broad-leaved trees; in wounds in living trees.

Chocolate Lenzites

Gloeophyllum sepiarium

SIZE:
¾-4 in. wide.

WHAT TO LOOK FOR:
cap thin, flexible, bright rusty brown (edge often white, yellow, or orange), hairy or smooth; underside with gills or pores; stem absent.

HABITAT:
on conifer logs, stumps, and lumber.

CLOSE-UP OF PORES

Willow Polypore

Daedalea confragosa

SIZE:
1-6 in. wide.

WHAT TO LOOK FOR:
cap gray to brown, often banded, leathery to rigid; underside white to brown, with gills or with round or irregular long pores; stem absent.

HABITAT:
on dead wood of broad-leaved trees; in wounds in living trees.

Honeycomb Bracket Fungus

Favolus alveolaris

SIZE:
½-4 in. wide; stem (if present) to ½ in. long.

WHAT TO LOOK FOR:
cap tough to brittle, red-yellow to brick-red (paler with age), often with small flattened scales; underside white, with texture like honeycomb; stem white.

HABITAT:
singly or in clusters on dead wood of broad-leaved trees.

CLOSE-UP OF PORES

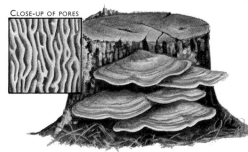

Teeth Fungi *Hydnaceae*

The fungi in this family can be soft, tough, or brittle. They also vary in appearance. Some have a cap with the teeth hanging from the underside; in others, the teeth make up most of the fungus. Spores are borne on the outside of each tooth. The Indian Paint Fungus, said to have been used by the Indians of the Pacific Northwest as a source of orange dye, causes heart rot in trees.

CLOSE-UP

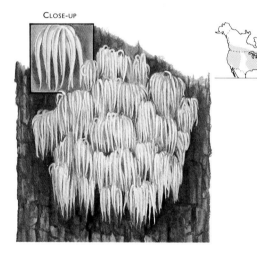

Coral Hydnum

Hericium coralloides

SIZE:
5-12 in. wide.

WHAT TO LOOK FOR:
numerous white branches (cream-colored with age), with iciclelike hanging spines on tips.

HABITAT:
on logs and dead trunks of broad-leaved trees; in wounds in living trees.

Indian Paint Fungus

Echinodontium tinctorium

SIZE:
1½-8 in. wide.

WHAT TO LOOK FOR:
cap hoof-shaped, woody, green-black or
dark brown, often cracked and moss-
covered; inside orange; teeth tough,
sometimes flattened, buff or brown-
gray.

HABITAT:
on living conifers.

Spreading Hedgehog Mushroom

Dentinum repandum

SIZE:
2-6 in. wide; stem 1-3 in. tall.

WHAT TO LOOK FOR:
cap dull to brownish orange, tan, or white; teeth white to cream or pale
salmon; stem white or colored like cap.

HABITAT:
under conifers or broad-leaved trees.

Bird's Nest Fungi *Nidulariaceae*

Each "egg" in these minuscule "nests" contains a multitude of spores. Rainwater splashes the eggs out of the nest, and their outer walls decay, spreading the spores and allowing them to germinate. Usually several nests appear together—sometimes even hundreds.

Striate Bird's Nest Fungus
Cyathus striatus

SIZE:
¼-½ in. wide; ¼-⅝ in. tall.

WHAT TO LOOK FOR:
bowl-shaped fungus; outside dark brown, hairy, inside whitish or black, striped; "eggs" inside bowl disklike, dark.

HABITAT:
in clusters on sticks and woody debris.

Earthstars *Geastraceae*

On an immature earthstar, the points of the star are firmly closed, and the structure resembles a puffball. With age, an outer layer, not found in true puffballs, splits open, revealing a sac that contains the spores. If pressed by a finger, the sac squirts the spores out in a cloud. Raindrops most likely cause the release of spores in more natural situations.

Earthstar

Geastrum triplex

SIZE:
2-4 in. wide, including points.

WHAT TO LOOK FOR:
central sac globular, light brown-gray, paler around opening; starlike points light gray-brown on top, darker below; spore "dust" brown.

HABITAT:
on soil and humus under broad-leaved trees.

Stinkhorns *Phallaceae*

An egg-shaped case resembling a puffball encloses the young stinkhorn. As the "egg" matures, the stinkhorn swells with water and lengthens rapidly—within the span of a few hours. The top of the mature stinkhorn is covered with a foul-smelling, spore-containing slime. Flies and beetles attracted to this transport stinkhorn spores to new areas.

Dog Stinkhorn

Mutinus caninus

SIZE:
2-4 in. tall.

WHAT TO LOOK FOR:
pink to red, foamy-looking stalk; tip tapered, with olive-green slime; remnants of oval "egg" at base.

HABITAT:
singly or in clusters on soil, humus, wood-chip mulch, or woody debris.

Eastern Stinkhorn

Phallus ravenelii

SIZE:
4-6 in. tall.

WHAT TO LOOK FOR:
cylindrical, slimy or dry fungus with gray- or olive-green head and ringed hole at tip; stem white, foamy-looking, usually with 1 or 2 thin brown rings; remnants of oval or round "egg" at base.

HABITAT:
on sawdust or wood debris.

Puffballs and False Puffballs *Lycoperdaceae and Relatives*

Considering the number of spores produced by a puffball's spongelike mass, it is surprising that these fungi are not everywhere underfoot. The highly prized Giant Puffball, for example, is believed to produce about 70 trillion spores, yet it is not a common species. Some, but not all, puffballs are choice eating. Even though they seem easily recognizable, there are poisonous lookalikes, such as the button (immature stage) of an amanita—another indication of the foolhardiness of dining on wild mushrooms without expert guidance.

Giant Puffball

Calvatia gigantea

SIZE:
6-20 in. wide.

WHAT TO LOOK FOR:
white globular fungus (turning yellow- or olive-brown with age, from center outward); attached to ground by short "cord."

HABITAT:
open grassy areas, woodland edges.

False Puffball

Scleroderma aurantium

SIZE:
1-4 in. wide.

WHAT TO LOOK FOR:
outside yellow-brown, cracked into small areas, each with dark wart; inside white (turning purple or black), firm (powdery with age); wall visible in cut section white, thick; spore "dust" black or brown.

HABITAT:
woods or parklike areas; near trees, logs, or stumps.

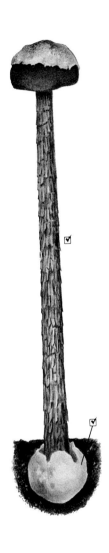

Desert Stalked Puffball

Battarraea phalloides

SIZE:
8-15 in. tall; spore sac 1-2 in. wide.

WHAT TO LOOK FOR:
spore sac egg-shaped, brown, atop long stem; stem brown, woody, shaggy; base cuplike; spore "dust" brown.

HABITAT:
in dry soil.

CROSS SECTION

False Truffle

Rhizopogon rubescens

SIZE:
½-2 in. wide.

WHAT TO LOOK FOR:
oval or round, white to yellow fungus (red spots with age); inside chambered, tough, rubbery, white (dingy yellow, then brown, with age).

HABITAT:
wholly or partially in needle duff or soil; usually under pines.

Pear-shaped Puffball

Lycoperdon pyriforme

SIZE:
¾-1½ in. wide.

WHAT TO LOOK FOR:
pear-shaped white to light brown fungus; inside white
(yellow, then olive-brown and powdery, with age); usually
attached to wood by white threads.

HABITAT:
in clusters on rotten logs and stumps; sawdust piles.

Slimy Stalked Puffball

Calostoma cinnabarina

Size:
1-2½ in. tall; spore sac ½-¾ in. wide.

WHAT TO LOOK FOR:
jelly coating on red spore sac, falling off in
pieces; raised pimple on top of sac; stem beneath
jelly red, netlike; spore "dust" yellow.

HABITAT:
in soil in low places in woods; along road banks.

Jelly Fungi *Tremellales*

The jellylike look of these fungi is deceptive, for they are actually so firm they can be cut only with a sharp object. Jelly fungi dry out for long periods, only to revive and resume growth when soaked with water. The Fairy Butter and Witches' Butter, for instance, are often prominent in winter woods when melting snow moistens the logs. Each time a jelly fungus revives, it produces new masses of spores over its wrinkled surface.

Fairy Butter
Dacrymyces palmatus

SIZE: ½-2½ in wide.

WHAT TO LOOK FOR: jellylike, tough fungus (soft and watery with age), yellow-orange, orange, or orange-red; looks like folded petals.

HABITAT: on conifer logs and stumps.

Witches' Butter
Tremella mesenterica

SIZE:
¾-4 in. wide; to 1½ in tall.

WHAT TO LOOK FOR:
firm, jellylike, orange to orange-yellow fungus with brainlike shape or broad folds.

HABITAT:
on logs, stumps, and dead branches of broad-leaved trees.

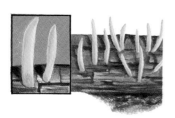

Horned Calocera
Calocera cornea

SIZE:
¼-¾ in. tall.

WHAT TO LOOK FOR:
firm, jellylike needles or horns (brittle when dry), sometimes with branches; yellow or orange-yellow.

HABITAT:
on dead trees.

Mushrooms 259

White Jelly Fungus

Pseudohydnum gelatinosum

SIZE: 1-2 in. wide; ¾-3 in. tall.

WHAT TO LOOK FOR:
cap translucent, whitish, jellylike, thick but pliable;
underside with white spines; stem (if present) short,
off-center.

HABITAT: on wood.

Yellow Jelly Fungus

Guepiniopsis alpinus

SIZE: ¼-½ in. wide.

WHAT TO LOOK FOR: yellow or orange
jellylike cup; narrow stem.

HABITAT:
in small clusters on conifer wood.

Black Witches' Butter

Exidia glandulosa

SIZE:
1-8 in. long.

WHAT TO LOOK FOR:
irregular jellylike masses, brown to black-brown
with brown warts (drying like black paint).

HABITAT:
on wood from broad-leaved trees.

Flask Fungi *Sphaeriales and Relatives*

Although they are probably the largest group of fungi, the flask fungi are generally inconspicuous, many being merely black specks on plant debris. Their unassuming appearance belies their importance; some species are notorious tree-killing parasites (those that cause Dutch elm disease and chestnut blight are examples). The powdery mildews, which give a moldy appearance to the leaves of lilacs, phlox, plums, cherries, and many weeds and grasses, are also flask fungi. The plants they live on look unsightly but are not permanently harmed by their presence.

Black Knot Fungus

Apiosporina morbosa

SIZE:
½-1½ in. wide; 1-12 in. long.

WHAT TO LOOK FOR:
dull olive-green (black with age), hard, generally cylindrical fungus; tapered, clublike, or irregularly lumpy.

HABITAT:
on twigs and branches of living or dead plum and cherry trees.

Dead Man's Fingers

Xylaria polymorpha

SIZE:
¾-4 in. tall.

WHAT TO LOOK FOR:
club-shaped or fingerlike fungus; outside black, rough; inside white, tough, woody.

HABITAT:
on decaying wood above ground or on buried wood.

Zoned Black Fungus

Daldinia concentrica

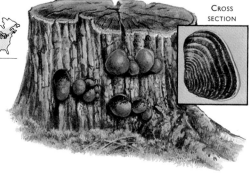

CROSS SECTION

SIZE: ¾-2 in. wide.

WHAT TO LOOK FOR: hard, round or half-round fungus; surface dull pink-brown (blackened by spore "dust" with age); concentric zones of gray and black visible when cut.

HABITAT: on stumps and logs of broad-leaved trees.

Orange-colored Cordyceps

Cordyceps militaris

SIZE:
¹⁄₁₆-¼ in. wide; ¾-3 in. tall.

WHAT TO LOOK FOR:
clublike cylindrical fungus; orange-buff or red-orange, with minute pimples on head.

HABITAT:
on dead moth or butterfly pupae buried in ground or on decayed wood.

Orange Hypomyces

Hypomyces lactifluorum

SIZE:
minute; coating other mushrooms.

WHAT TO LOOK FOR:
orange or orange-red coating, with deep orange or red dots; covers entire mushroom or only gills and stem; makes gills visible only as faint ridges.

HABITAT:
on certain mushrooms (russulas and lactarii).

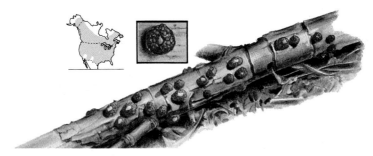

Red Pimple Fungus

Nectria cinnabarina

SIZE: about 1/16 in. wide.

WHAT TO LOOK FOR: small pink to orange-red cushion (dark red with age).

HABITAT: in groups on sticks or dead branches of living trees.

Cup Fungi *Pezizales and Relatives*

The fungi in this group vary widely in appearance. The morels and false morels on pages 267 through 269, for example, bear little resemblance to the small, colorful cups shown on pages 263 through 266. What they have in common is their microscopic spore sacs, borne on the upper or inside surface of the cups or, in the morels, on the entire outer surface. Some spring-fruiting morels are prized delicacies, but mushroom hunters should beware: false morels and other poisonous relatives appear during the same season.

Gray Urn

Urnula craterium

SIZE:
1-3 in. wide; 2-5 in. tall.

WHAT TO LOOK FOR:
urn or deep cup; inside dark brown to black, outside dark gray to brown (black with age).

HABITAT:
in clusters on or near sticks and logs of broad-leaved trees.

Orange Peel

Caloscypha fulgens

Size: ½-2 in. wide.

What to look for: cup-shaped fungus, often split or lopsided; inside yellow to orange, outside with blue-green tints or stains.

Habitat: in clusters in wet places under conifers.

Scarlet Cup

Sarcoscypha coccinea

Size: ½-2 in. wide.

What to look for: bright scarlet cup (whitish on outside); stem very short or absent.

Habitat: on hardwood sticks.

Confusing Peziza

Peziza badioconfusa

Size: 1-4 in. wide.

What to look for: shallow cup; inside brown or red-brown, outside dull yellow-brown (black all over with age).

Habitat: on soil or humus or beside logs and stumps.

Orange Fairy Cup

Aleuria aurantia

SIZE: ¾-4 in. wide.

WHAT TO LOOK FOR: shallow cup or saucer; inside bright red-orange, outside white, translucent.

HABITAT: in clusters on packed soil in dirt roads and paths.

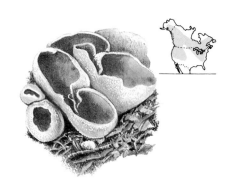

Pink Crown

Sarcosphaera crassa

SIZE:
1-4½ in. wide.

WHAT TO LOOK FOR:
deep cup with crownlike edge; inside gray-lilac to pink, outside white; stem (if present) short, thick.

HABITAT:
woods; wholly or partly buried in soil.

Blue-green Cup Fungus

Chlorociboria aeruginascens

SIZE:
¼-1½ in. wide.

WHAT TO LOOK FOR:
shallow, dull blue-green cup; very short stem.

HABITAT:
in clusters on logs or dead branches of conifers.

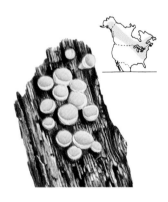

Yellow Cup Fungus

Bisporella citrina

SIZE:
⅛-¼ in. wide.

WHAT TO LOOK FOR:
shallow, bright yellow disk or cup, often fused
with others into large mass.

HABITAT:
in clusters on dead wood of broad-leaved trees.

Yellow Leotia

Leotia lubrica

½-1½ in. wide; stem ½-2½ in. tall.

WHAT TO LOOK FOR:
oval or cushion-shaped cap on
club-shaped stem; cap and stem
slimy, dingy yellow, buff, or brown
(sometimes with olive tint).

HABITAT:
in clusters on soil or moss in woods.

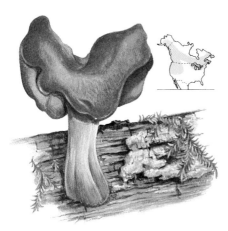

Bay Gyromitra

Gyromitra infula

SIZE:
1-5 in. wide; stem 1-4½ in. tall.

WHAT TO LOOK FOR:
cap generally saddle-shaped, sometimes slightly wrinkled, buff or dark
brown or red-brown; stem whitish or
tinted brown.

HABITAT:
on rotting conifer wood; occasionally
in rich woodland soils.

CROSS
SECTION

Early Morel
Verpa bohemica

SIZE:
½-1 in. wide; 3-4 in. tall.

WHAT TO LOOK FOR:
cap bell-shaped, yellow-brown, attached at top of stem (bottom edge free), wrinkled or folded, with deep elongated pits; stem hollow, whitish, yellow, or tan.

HABITAT:
wet areas.

Common Morel
Morchella esculenta

SIZE:
1-2 in. wide; 1½-4 in. tall.

WHAT TO LOOK FOR:
cap continuous with stem, gray or light yellow to brown with rounded ridges and rounded or irregular pits; stem white.

HABITAT:
old orchards; broad-leaved forests; grassy areas; low wet areas; near recently dead elms; occasionally in gardens.

CROSS
SECTION

Elfin Saddle

Helvella lacunosa

SIZE:
½-2 in. wide; stem 1½-5 in. tall.

WHAT TO LOOK FOR:
cap saddle-shaped, slightly wrinkled or folded, gray; stem pale gray, with deep channels.

HABITAT:
on ground in woods; sometimes on decaying wood.

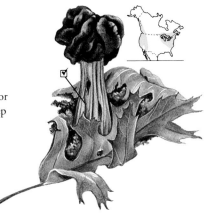

False Morel

Gyromitra esculenta

SIZE:
1½-4 in. wide; stem 1-3 in. tall.

WHAT TO LOOK FOR:
cap wrinkled, folded (like a brain), irregularly shaped, brown or red-brown, lacking pits; stem whitish.

HABITAT:
under conifers.

Index

Abies balsamea, 30
  concolor, 30
  fraseri, 29
  grandis, 30
  lasiocarpa, 29
  magnifica, 29
Acacia greggii, 88
Acacia, 88
Acer circinatum, 98
  glabrum, 99
  macrophyllum, 101
  negundo, 100
  pensylvanicum, 100
  platanoides, 96
  rubrum, 97
  saccharinum, 98
  saccharum, 97
Acetabularia crenulata, 182
Adder's Tongue, 138
Adenostoma fasciculatum, 117
  sparsifolium, 117
Adiantum capillusveneris, 140
  jordanii, 142
  pedatum, 140
Aesculus glabra, 95
  hippocastanum, 95
  octandra, 95
Agar Weed, 185
Agaric, Fly, 203
Agaricus arvensis, 231
  campestris, 232
  placomyces, 232
Ailanthus altissima, 102
Ailanthus, 102
Alder, 68
  Red (Oregon), 68
Aleuria aurantia, 265
Algae, 182-187
  Bang's Primitive Red, 186
  Cartilaginous Red, 184
  Green Thread, 183
  Rosy-bladed Red, 186
  Tube, 182
  Vesselled Red, 187
  Wormlike Red, 185
Allspice, 110
  Carolina, 110
  Smooth, 110
Alnus rubra, 68
Amanita caesarea, 204
  citrina, 205
  muscaria, 203
  pantherina, 203
  phalloides, 202
  rubescens, 204
  vaginata, 205
  virosa, 202
Amanita, 202-205
  Napkin, 205
  Panther, 203
Amelanchier arborea, 83
Andromeda glaucophylla, 115
Anthoceros laevis, 180

Apiosporina morbosa, 261
Apple, 79
  Oregon Crab, 79
  Sweet Crab, 79
Aralia hispida, 105
  spinosa, 105
Aralia, 105
Arborvitae, 35
  Eastern, 35
  Giant, 35
Arbutus menziesii, 78
Arctostaphylos glauca, 117
  uva-ursi, 117
Armillaria ponderosa, 218
Armillariella mellea, 217
Artemisia stelleriana, 130
  tridentata, 130
Ash, 82, 102-104
  Black, 104
  Green, 104
  Mountain-, 82
  Prickly-, 103
  Singleleaf, 104
  Wafer-, 102
  White, 104
Asimina triloba, 40
Asimina, 40
Aspen,
  Bigtooth, 75
  Quaking, 75
Asplenium montanum, 152
  platyneuron, 151
  ruta-muraria, 150
  trichomanes, 150
Asplenosorus pinnatifidus, 151
Asterophora lycoperdoides, 216
Asterophora, Parastic, 216
Athyrium filix-femina, 154
  pycnocarpon, 153
  thelypterioides, 154
Atrichum undulatum, 179
Atriplex canescens, 112
  confertifolia, 112
Avicennia germinans, 105
Azalea, Flame, 115
Azolla caroliniana, 166

Baccharis halimifolia, 131
Baccharis, 131
Baldcypress, 34
Bangiales, 186
Basswood, American, 70
Battarraea phalloides, 257
Bayberry, 111
  Northern, 111
  Southern, 111
Bazzania trilobata, 181
Bearberry, 117
Beech, 55
  American, 55
Betula alleghaniensis, 66
  lenta, 66
  nigra, 66
    papyrifera, 67
Birch, 66-67
  Paper (Canoe), 67

River (Red), 67
  Sweet (Black or Cherry), 66
  Yellow, 66
Bisporella citrina, 266
Blackberry, Highbush, 120
Blackgum, 93
Black-mangrove, 105
Bladdernut, 126
  American, 126
  Sierra, 126
Blechnum spicant, 163
Blewit, Wood, 218
Blueberry, 118
  Highbush, 118
  Lowbush, 118
Blueblossom, 124
Blusher, 204
Bolbitii, 233
Boletaceae, 244
Bolete, 243-246
  Admirable, 245
  American Yellow, 244
  Bitter, 246
  Greville's, 244
  King, 246
  Painted, 244
  Two-colored, 245
Boletinus, Hollow-stemmed, 243
Boletus bicolor, 245
  edulis, 246
  mirabilis, 245
Botrychium virginianum, 138
Boxelder, 100
Bracken, 146
Brake,
  American Rock, 141
  Purple Cliff, 143
  Smooth Cliff, 143
  Spiny Cliff, 144
Bramble, 120
Brick Top, 227
British Soldiers, 196
Brownie Cap, 233
Bryopsis corticulans, 182
Bryum argenteum, 177
Buckbrush, 124
Buckeye, 95
  Ohio (Stinking), 95
  Yellow, 95
Buckthorn, 93
  Carolina, 93
  Cascara, 93
  European, 93
Burningbush, 125
  Eastern, 125
Butternut, 51
Buttonbush, 127

Cactus, Giant, 70
California-laurel, 42
Calocera cornea, 259
Calocera, Horned, 259
Caloscypha fulgens, 264
Calostoma cinnabarina, 258
Calvatia gigantea, 256
Calycanthus fertilis, 110
  floridus, 110

Camptosorus rhizophyllus, 153
Cantharellus cibarius, 237
   lateritius, 238
   tubaeformis, 239
Cantharellus, Tubed, 239
Carpinus caroliniana, 69
Carya cordiformis, 52
   illinoensis, 54
   ovata, 53
tomentosa, 54
Castanea dentata, 57
   pumila, 56
   sativa, 57
Castanopsis chrysophylla, 56
   sempervirens, 56
Catalpa bignonioides, 106
   speciosa, 106
Catalpa, 106
   Northern, 106
   Southern, 106
Catclaw, Gregg (Acacia), 88
Ceanothus americanus, 124
   cuneatus, 124
   thyrsiflorus, 124
Ceanothus, 124
Cedar (tree), 35, 39
   Eastern Red-, 39
   Northern White-, 35
   Western Red-, 35
Cedar, Running (clubmoss), 168
Celtis laevigata, 46
   occidentalis, 46
Cephalanthus occidentalis, 127
Ceramiales, 187
Ceratodon purpureus, 175
Cercidium floridum, 89
   microphyllum, 89
Cercis canadensis, 85
   occidentalis, 85
Cercocarpus betuloides, 85
   ledifolius, 85
Cercocarpus, 85
   Birchleaf, 85
   Curlleaf, 85
Cereus giganteus, 70
Cereus, 70
Chamaecyparis lawsoniana, 36
   thyoides, 36
Chamaedaphne calyculata, 116
Chamise, 117
Chanterelle, 237-238
   False, 221
   Gill-less, 238
   Shaggy, 238
Cheilanthes feei, 141
   gracillima, 142
   lanosa, 142
Chenille Weed, 187
Cherry, 80-81
   Black, 81
   Choke-, 81
   Pin (Fire), 80
Chestnut, 57, 95
   American, 57
   Horse-, 95
   Spanish, 57
Chilopsis linearis, 108

Chinkapin, 56
   Allegheny, 56
   Giant, 56
   Sierra, 56
Chionanthus virginicus, 106
Chlorociboria aeruginascens, 266
Chlorophyllum molybdites, 207
Chlorosplenium aeruginosum, 268
Chokecherry, 81
Chondrus crispus, 184
Chorda filum, 189
Christmas-berry, 121
Chrysothamnus nauseosus, 130
Cladina rangiferina, 195
Cladonia cristatella, 196
   pyxidata, 196
   verticillata, 196
Clavaria, 240-242
   Crowned, 241
   Golden, 241
Clavariaceae, 241
Clavariadelphus truncatus, 240
Clavicorona pyxidata, 241
Clavulina cinerea, 242
Clavulinopsis fusiformis, 241
Climacium dendroides, 177
Clitocybe clavipes, 215
   nuda, 218
Clitocybe, Club-footed, 215
Clover, 167
   Hairy Water, 167
   Water, 167
Club-moss, 167-169
   Bog, 168
   Shining, 167
   Tree, 169
Coffeetree, Kentucky, 86
Collybia, Rooting, 220
Comptonia peregrina, 111
Conocybe tenera, 233
Coprinus atramentarius, 229
   comatus, 230
   micaceus, 230
Coral Fungus, 240-242
   Gray, 242
   Spindle, 241
Coralbean, 90
   Southeastern, 90
   Southwestern, 90
Cord Weed, Smooth, 189
Cordyceps militaris, 262
Cordyceps, Orange-colored, 262
Coriolus versicolor, 248
Cornus alternifolia, 123
   florida, 94
   nuttallii, 94
   stolonifera, 123
Cortinarius armillatus, 235
   cinnamomeus, 236
   semisanguineus, 236
   violaceus, 236
Cortinarii, 234-236
   Cinnamon, 236
   Red-gilled, 236
   Red-zoned, 235
   Violet, 236
Corylus comuta, 112

Cottonwood, Eastern, 74
Cranberry, 118
Crataegus pruinosa, 84
Craterellus fallax, 237
Craterellus, Deceptive, 237
Creosote Bush, 125
Cryptogramma acrostichoides, 141
Cucumbertree, 45
Cupressus arizonica, 37
   macrocarpa, 37
Currant, 121
   American Black, 121
Cyathea, 146
Cyathus striatus, 254
Cypress, 34, 36-37
   Arizona, 37
   Bald-, 34
   Lawson, 36
   Monterey, 37
Cyrilla racemiflora, 113
Cyrilla, Swamp, 113
Cryptogramma acrostichoides, 141
Cystopteris bulbifera, 155
   fragilis, 155

Dacrymyces palmatus, 259
Daedalea confragosa, 251
Daldinia concentrica, 262
Dalea spinosa, 88
Dalea, 88
Dasya pedicellata, 187
Dead Man's Fingers, 261
Death Cup, 202
Dennstaedtia punctilobula, 146
Dentinum repandum, 253
Desert-willow, 108
Destroying Angel, 202
Devils-walkingstick, 105
Dicksonia, 146
Dicranum scoparium, 176
Diospyros texana, 78
   virginiana, 78
Dogwood, 94, 123
   Alternate-leaf, 123
   Flowering, 94
   Pacific, 94
   Red-osier, 123
Douglas-fir, 31
Dryopteris carthusiana, 163
   cristata, 162
   filix-mas, 161
   goldiana, 161
   marginalis, 162
Dulse, 186
Dusty-miller, 130

Earthstar, 254
Echinodontium tinctorium, 253
Elder, 128
   American (Elderberry), 128
   Pacific Red, 128
Elfin Saddle, 269
Elm, 48-49
   American (White), 48
   Slippery, 48
   Winged (Wahoo), 49

Entoloma abortivum, 226
  salmoneum, 225
  sinuatum, 225
Entoloma, 225-226
  Abortive, 226
  Livid, 225
  Salmon, 225
Equisetum arvense, 172
  fluviatile, 173
  hyemale, 173
  laevigatum, 172
Erythrina flabelliformis, 90
  herbacea, 90
Eucalyptus globulus, 82
Eucalyptus, Bluegum, 82
Euonymus atropurpureus, 125
Evernia mesomorpha, 197
Exidia glandulosa, 260

Fagus grandifolia, 55
Fairy Butter, 259
Fairy Cup, Orange, 265
Fairy Ring, 224
Favolus alveolaris, 251
Fern, 136-167
  American Climbing, 139
  Appalachian Bristle, 144
  Broad Beech, 148
  Bulbet, 155
  Christmas, 158
  Cinnamon, 137
  Climbing, 139
  Crested Wood, 162
  Curly Grass, 139
  Deer, 163
  Filmy, 144
  Fragile (Brittle), 155
  Giant Chain, 165
  Glade, 153
  Goldback, 141
  Goldie's Wood, 161
  Grape, 138
  Hairy Lip, 142
  Hammock, 147
  Hart's-Tongue, 152
  Hartford, 139
  Hay-scented, 146
  Interrupted, 137
  Japanese Climbing, 139
  Lace, 142
  Lady, 154
  Long Beech, 148
  Maidenhair, 140
  Male, 161
  Marginal Wood, 162
  Marsh, 149
  Mosquito, 166
  Netted Chain, 164
  New York, 149
  Northern Holly, 158
  Oak, 165
  Ostrich, 160
  Parsley, 141
  Polypody, 145
  Rattlesnake, 138
  Resurrection, 145
  Royal, 136

Sensitive, 159
Silvery Glade, 154
Slender Lip, 141
Southern Maidenhair, 140
Sweet-, 111
Toothed Wood, 163
Tree, 146
Virginia Chain, 164
Walking, 153
Western Sword, 159
Filbert, Beaked, 112
Fir, 29-31
  Balsam, 30
  California Red, 29
  Douglas-, 31
  Fraser, 29
  Grand (Lowland White), 30
  Subalpine, 29
  True, 29
  White, 30
Fissidens grandifrons, 174
Flammulina velutipes, 221
Fomes fomentarius, 250
Fomes, Bracket, 250
Fomitopsis pinicola, 250
Forestiera acuminata, 126
Forestiera, 126
Fouquieria splendens, 114
Fraxinus americana, 104
  anomala, 104
  nigra, 104
  pennsylvanica, 104
Fringetree, 106
Fucus vesiculosus, 191
Funaria hygrometrica, 176
Fungus, 198-269
  Artist's, 247
  Bird's Nest, 254
  Black Knot, 261
  Blue-green Cup, 266
  Coral, 240-242
  Cup, 263
  Flask, 261-263
  Honeycomb Bracket, 251
  Indian Paint, 253
  Jelly, 260
  Pore, 247-252
  Red Belt, 250
  Red Pimple, 263
  Striate Bird's Nest, 254
  Teeth, 252-253
  White Jelly, 260
  Yellow Cup, 266
  Yellow Jelly, 260
  Zoned Black, 262

Galerina autumnalis, 235
Galerina, Autumn, 235
Ganoderma applanatum, 247
  tsugae, 248
Geastrum triplex, 254
Gelidium robustum, 185
Gigartina stellata, 184
Ginkgo biloba, 40
Ginkgo, 40
Gleditsia aquatica, 90
  triacanthos, 90

Gloeophyllum sepiarium, 251
Golden Trumpets, 215
Goldilocks, 178
Gomphidius glutinosus, 226
Gomphidius, Slimy, 226
Gomphus clavatus, 239
  floccosus, 238
Gooseberry, 121
Gordonia lasianthus, 68
Gordonia, 68
Gray Urn, 263
Greasewood, 117
Grifola frondosa, 249
Grimmia alpicola, 176
Grisette, 205
Groundsel-tree, 131
Guepiniopsis alpinus, 260
Gulfweed, Attached, 191
Gymnocarpium dryopteris, 165
Gymnocladus dioicus, 86
Gyromitra esculenta, 269
  infula, 267
Gyromitra, Bay, 267

Hackberry, 46
Halesia carolina, 119
Hamamelis virginiana, 109
Hawthorn, 84
  Frosted, 84
Hazel, Beaked, 112
He-huckleberry, 113
Helvella lacunosa, 269
Hemlock, 12
  Carolina, 12
  Eastern, 12
  Mountain, 12
  Western, 12
Hen of the Woods, 249
Hercules-club, 103
Hericium corralloides, 252
Heteromeles arbutifolia, 121
Hickory, 52-54
  Bitternut, 52
  Mockernut, 54
  Shagbark, 53
Hobblebush, 129
Holly, American, 92
Honey-ball, 127
Honeylocust, 90
Honeysuckle, 128
  Fly, 128
  Tatarian, 128
Hop-hornbeam, 69
  Eastern, 69
Hoptree, 102
  California, 102
  Common, 102
Hornbeam, 69
  American (Blue-beech), 69
  Hop-, 69
Hornwort, Common, 180
Horsechestnut, 95
Horse-sugar, 77
Horsetail, 172
  Field, 172
  Water, 173
Hydnum, Coral, 252

Hygrophoropsis aurantiaca, 221
Hygrophorus conicus, 208
　miniatus, 209
　psittacinus, 208
　russula, 209
Hygrophorus, 208-209
　Cone-shaped, 208
　Parrot, 208
　Russula, 209
　Vermilion, 209
Hypnum imponens, 179
Hypomyces lactifluorum, 262
Hypomyces, Orange, 262

Ilex cassine, 92
　decidua, 92
　opaca, 92
　verticillata, 92
　vomitoria, 92
Indigobush, 88
Inky Cap, 229-230
　Glistening, 230
Inocybe fastigiata, 235
Inocybe, Clustered, 235
Isoetes echinospora, 171

Jack-o'-lantern, 221
Joshua-tree, 108
Juglans cinerea, 51
　nigra, 51
　regia, 50
Juniper, 38
　Common (Dwarf), 38
　Creeping, 38
　Oneseed, 38
　Utah (Bigberry), 39
Juniperus communis, 38
　horizontalis, 38
　monosperma, 38
　osteosperma, 39
　virginiana, 39

Kalmia angustifolia, 116
　latifolia, 116
　polifolia, 116
Kelp, 188, 190
　Bull, 188
　Giant, 190

Labrador Tea, 114
Laccaria laccata, 223
Laccaria, Waxy, 223
Lactarius deceptivus, 210
　deliciosus, 211
　indigo, 210
　volemus, 211
Lactarius, 210-211
　Blue, 210
　Delicious, 211
　Orange-brown, 211
Laguncularia racemosa, 91
Lambkill, 116
Laminaria saccharina, 189
Larch, 24
　Eastern (Tamarack), 24
　Subalpine, 24
　Western, 24

Larix laricina, 24
　lyallii, 24
　occidentalis, 24
Larrea tridentata, 125
Laurel, 116
　Bog, 116
　California-, 42
　Great, 115
　Mountain, 116
Laver, 186
Leatherleaf, 116
Leatherwood, 113
Ledum groenlandicum, 114
Ledum, 114
Lentinus lepideus, 213
Lentinus, Scaly, 213
Lenzites, Chocolate, 251
Leotia lubrica, 267
Leotia Yellow, 267
Lepiota americana, 206
　lutea, 206
　procera, 206
　rachodes, 207
Lepiota, 206-207
　Blushing, 206
　Shaggy, 207
　Smooth, 206
　Yellow, 206
Letharia vulpina, 197
Lettuce, Sea, 183
Leucoagaricus naucinus, 206
Leucobryum glaucum, 174
Lichen, 192-197
　Beard, 195
　Cracked Shield, 194
　Dog, 192
　Flabby, 197
　Ladder, 196
　Lung, 193
　Map, 193
　Orange Star, 193
　Reindeer, 195
　Toadskin, 194
　Wolf, 197
Lily-of-the-valley-Tree, 76
Lindera benzoin, 110
　melissaefolium, 110
Liquidambar styraciflua, 43
Liriodendron chinense, 41
　tulipifera, 41
Lithocarpus densiflorus, 55
Liverwort, 180-181
　Braided, 181
　Common, 180
Lobaria pulmonaria, 193
Loblolly-bay, 68
Locust, 87, 90
　Black, 87
　Honey-, 90
　Water-, 90
Lonicera canadensis, 128
　tatarica, 128
Lycoperdon pyriforme, 258
Lycopodium clavatum, 168
　digitatum, 169
　inundatum, 168
　lucidulum, 167

　obscurum, 169
Lygodium japonicum, 139
　palmatum, 139

Maclura pomifera, 49
Macrocystis pyrifera, 190
Madrone, Pacific, 78
Magnolia acuminata, 45
　grandiflora, 44
　virginiana, 45
Magnolia, 44-45
　Cucumber, 45
　Southern (Evergreen), 44
　Swamp, 45
Mahogany, Mountain-, 85
Maidenhair
　California, 142
　Northern, 140
　Southern, 140
Maidenhair Tree, 40
Malus coronaria, 79
　fusca, 79
　sylvestris, 79
Mangrove, 91
　Black-, 105
　Red, 91
　White-, 91
Manzanita, Bigberry, 117
Maple, 96-101
　Ashleaf (Boxelder), 100
　Bigleaf, 101
　Dwarf, 99
　Norway, 96
　Oregon, 101
　Red (Swamp), 97
　Rocky Mountain, 99
　Silver, 98
　Striped (Moosewood), 100
　Sugar, 97
　Vine, 98
Marasmius oreades, 224
　rotula, 217
Marchantia polymorpha, 180
Marsilea vestita, 167
Matteuccia struthiopteris, 160
Merlin's Grass, 171
Mermaid's Wineglass, 182
Merman's Shaving Brush, 182
Mesquite, Honey, 87
Milky Cap, Cottony-margined, 210
Mnium cuspidatum, 178
Mnium, Woodsy, 178
Moosewood, 100
Morchella esculenta, 268
Morel, 268-269
　Common, 268
　Early, 268
　False, 269
Morus alba, 47
　nigra, 47
　rubra, 47
Moss, 174-179
　Broom, 176
　Burned Ground (Purple), 175
　Club-, 167-169
　Cord, 176

Moss, *cont.*
  Delicate Fern, 178
  Feather, 179
  Four-tooth, 179
  Haircap, 178
  Irish (seaweed), 184
  Red Spoonleaf Peat, 175
  Reindeer (lichen), 195
  Rock, 176
  Sea (seaweed), 182
  Silver, 177
  Spike-, 170-171
  Spineleaf, 179
  Star, 178
  Tree, 177
  Water Fern, 174
  White Cushion, 174
Mountain-ash, 82
  American, 82
  European, 82
Mountain-mahogany, 85
Mulberry, 47
  Black, 47
  Red, 47
  White, 47
Musci, 174
Mushroom, 198-269
  Caesar's, 204
  Cauliflower, 242
  Club, 240
  Flat-topped, 232
  Green Gill, 207
  Haymaker's, 229
  Honey, 217
  Horse, 231
  Little Wheel, 217
  Meadow, 231-232
  Oyster, 216
  Parasol, 206
  Pine, 218
  Split-gilled, 214
  Spreading Hedgehog, 253
  Tube, 243-246
  Winter, 221
Mutinus caninus, 255
Mycena haematopus, 219
  leaiana, 219
  pura, 219
Mycena, 219, 221
  Bleeding, 219
  Clean, 219
  Golden, 219
Myrica cerifera, 111
  pensylvanica, 111
Myrtle, 42, 111
  Oregon-, 42
  Wax-, 111

*N*aematoloma capnoides, 228
  fasciculare, 228
  sublateritium, 227
Nannyberry, 129
Nectria cinnabarina, 263
Nemalionales, 185
Neptune's Girdle, 186
Nereocystis luetkeana, 188
New Jersey Tea, 124

Nidulariaceae, 255
Nyssa aquatica, 93
  sylvatica, 93

*O*ak, 58-65
  Blackjack (Barren), 61
  Bur (Mossycup), 65
  California Black, 62
  Chestnut (Rock), 64
  Coast Live, 60
  Live, 62
  Northern Red, 58
  Pin (Swamp), 60
  Post, 63
  Scarlet, 59
  Valley (California White), 64
  White, 63
  Willow (Peach), 61
Ocotillo, 114
Old Man of the Woods, 245
Old-mans-beard, 106
Omphalotus olearius, 221
Onoclea sensibilis, 159
Ophioglossum vulgatum, 138
Orange Peel, 264
Oregon-myrtle, 42
Osage-orange, 49
Osmunda cinnamomea, 137
  claytoniana, 137
  regalis, 136
Ostrya virginiana, 69
Oudemansiella radicata, 220
Oxydendrum arboreum, 76
Oxyporus nobilissimus, 247

*P*alm, 107
  Florida Royal-, 107
  Sea (seaweed), 190
Palmae, 107
Palmetto, 107, 131
  Cabbage, 107
  Saw-, 131
Paloverde, 89
  Blue, 89
  Yellow, 89
Parmelia sulcata, 194
Pawpaw, 40
Paxillus atrotomentosus, 233
  involutus, 233
Paxillus, 233
  Black-footed, 233
  Involute, 233
Pecan, 54
Pellaea atropurpurea, 143
  glabella, 143
  truncata, 144
Peltigera canina, 192
Penicillus capitatus, 182
Persimmon, 78
  Common, 78
  Texas, 78
Peziza badioconfusa, 264
Peziza, Confusing, 264
Phallus ravenellii, 255
Pholiota squarrosoides, 234
Pholiota, Scaly, 234
Phyllitis scolopendrium, 152

Picea abies, 26
  engelmannii, 27
  glauca, 27
  mariana, 25
  pungens, 25
  rubens, 25
  sitchensis, 28
Pig's Ears, 239
Pine, 14
  Bristlecone, 15
  Eastern White, 16
  Ground (clubmoss), 168
  Jack, 17
  Limber, 14
  Loblolly, 23
  Lodgepole, 19
  Longleaf, 18
  Monterey, 14
  Pitch, 23
  Ponderosa (Western Yellow), 20
  Red (Norway), 19
  Running (clubmoss), 169
  Scotch (Scots), 21
  Shortleaf, 20
  Slash, 22
  Sugar, 15
  Western White, 14
Pink Crown, 265
Pinus aristata, 15
  banksiana, 17
  contorta, 19
  echinata, 20
  edulis, 17
  elliottii, 22
  flexilis, 14
  lambertiana, 15
  monticola, 14
  palustris, 18
  ponderosa, 20
  radiata, 14
  resinosa, 19
  rigida, 23
  strobus, 16
  sylvestris, 21
  taeda, 23
Pinyon, 17
Pipes, 173
Pityrogramma triangularis, 141
Planetree, 50
  London, 50
  Oriental, 50
Platanus occidentalis, 50
  orientalis, 50
  racemosa, 50
  Platycerium, 145
Pleurotus ostreatus, 216
Plum, American, 80
Pluteaceae, 225
Poison Sumac, 127
Polypodium polypodioides, 145
  virginianum, 145
Polypody, Common, 145
Polyporaceae, 248
Polypore, 247-251
  Hemlock, 248
  Many-colored, 248
  Noble, 247

Sulphur, 249
Willow, 251
Polyporus sulphureus, 249
Polystichum acrostichoides, 158
  lonchitis, 158
  munitum, 159
Polytrichum commune, 178
Poplar, 74-75
  Balsam, 75
  Yellow-, 41
Populus balsamifera, 75
  deltoides, 74
  grandidentata, 75
  tremuloides, 75
Porphyra perforata, 186
Port-Orford-cedar, 36
Possumhaw, 92
Postelsia palmaeformis, 190
Prickly-ash, 103
  Common, 103
Privet, Swamp-, 126
Prosopis glandulosa, 87
Prunus americana, 80
  pensylvanica, 80
  serotina, 81
  virginiana, 81
Psathyrella foenisecii, 229
Pseudohydnum gelatinosum, 260
Pseudotsuga menziesii, 31
Psilocybe, Cuban, 228
Psilocybe cubensis, 228
Ptelea crenulata, 102
  trifoliata, 102
Pteridium aquilinum, 146
Puffball, 256-212
  Desert Stalked, 257
  False, 256
  Giant, 256
  Pear-shaped, 258
  Slimy Stalked, 258
Pyxie Cups, 196

Quercus agrifolia, 60
  alba, 63
  coccinea, 59
  kelloggii, 62
  lobata, 64
  macrocarpa, 65
  marilandica, 61
  palustris, 60
  phellos, 61
  prinus, 64
  rubra, 58
  stellata, 63
  virginiana, 62
Quillwort, Spiny-spored, 171

Rabbitbrush, 130
Ramaria aurea, 240
Red Weed, Tufted, 184
Redbud, 85
  California, 85
  Eastern, 85
Redcedar,
  Eastern, 39
  Western, 35
Redgum, 43

Redshank, 117
Redwood, 33
Rhamnus caroliniana, 93
  cathartica, 93
  purshiana, 93
Rhizocarpon geographicum, 193
Rhizophora mangle, 91
Rhizopogon rubescens, 257
Rhododendron calendulaceum, 115
  maximum, 115
Rhododendron, Rosebay, 115
Rhodophylls, 225-226
Rhodymenia palmata, 186
Rhus integrifolia, 101
  typhina, 101
Ribes americanum, 121
Ricciocarpus natans, 181
Robinia pseudoacacia, 87
Rock Tripe, 194
Rockweed, 191
Rosa multiflora, 122
  setigera, 122
Rose, 122
  Multiflora, 122
  Prairie, 122
Rosemary, Bog, 115
Royalpalm, Florida, 107
Roystonea elata, 107
Rubus alleghaniensis, 120
Rue, Wall, 150
Rush, 172-173
  Scouring-, 173
  Smooth Scouring-, 172
Russula brevipes, 212
  emetica, 212
Russula, 210, 212
  Pungent, 212
  Short-stemmed, 212

Sabal palmetto, 107
Sagebrush, Common, 130
Saguaro, 70
Salix amygdaloides, 72
  babylonica, 73
  discolor, 72
  exigua, 71
  nigra, 73
Saltbush, Four-wing, 112
Salvinia minima, 166
Sambucus callicarpa, 128
  canadensis, 128
Sapindus drummondii, 94
  saponaria, 94
Sarcoscypha coccinea, 264
Sarcosphaera crassa, 265
Sargassum filipendula, 191
Sarsaparilla, Bristly, 105
Sassafras albidum, 42
Sassafras, 42
Saw-palmetto, 131
Scarlet Cup, 264
Schizaea pusilla, 139
Schizophyllum commune, 214
Scleroderma aurantium, 256
Seaweeds, 182-190
Selaginella apoda, 170
  densa, 171

  rupestris, 170
Sequoia sempervirens, 33
Sequoia, Giant, 32
Sequoiadendron giganteum, 32
Serenoa repens, 131
Serviceberry, Downy, 83
Shadbush, 83
Shad-scale, 112
Shaggy Mane, 230
Silverbell, Carolina, 119
Siphonales, 182
Slippery Jack, 243
Smokethorn (Smoketree), 88
Snowbell, Bigleaf, 119
Soapberry, 94
  Western, 94
  Wingleaf, 94
Sorbus americana, 82
Sourgum, 93
Sourwood, 76
Spangles, Water, 166
Spanish-bayonet, 108
Sparassis radicata, 242
Sparkleberry, Tree, 118
Sphaeriales, 263
Sphagnum magellanicum, 175
Spicebush, 110
  Hairy, 110
Spike-moss, 170-171
  Meadow, 170
  Rock, 170
  Rocky Mountain, 171
Spleenwort, 147, 150-153
  Ebony, 151
  Lobed, 151
  Maidenhair, 150
  Mountain, 152
  Narrow-leaved, 153
Spruce, 25-28
  Black, 25
  Blue, 25
  Engelmann, 27
  Norway, 26
  Red, 25
  Sitka, 28
  White, 27
Staphylea bolanderi, 126
  trifolia, 126
Stinkhorn, 255
  Dog, 255
  Eastern, 255
Strobilomyces floccopus, 24
Stropharia, 227
Strophariaceae, 228
Styrax grandifolius, 119
Sugar Wrack, 189
Sugarberry, 46
Suillus americanus, 244
  cavipes, 243
  grevillei, 244
  luteus, 243
  pictus, 244
Sulphur Top, 228
Sumac, 101
  Lemonade, 101
  Poison, 127
  Staghorn, 101

Swamp-privet, 126
Sweetbay, 45
Sweet-fern, 111
Sweetgum, 43
Sweetleaf, 77
Sweetshrub, 110
Sycamore, California, 50
Symplocos tinctoria, 77

Tamarack (Eastern Larch), 24
Tanoak, 55
Taxodium distichum, 34
Taxus brevifolia, 13
    canadensis, 13
Tea, 114, 124
    Labrador, 114
    New Jersey, 124
Tetraphis pellucida, 179
Thelypteris hexagonoptera, 148
    kunthii, 147
    noveboracensis, 149
    palustris, 149
    phegopteris, 148
Thuidium delicatulum, 178
Thuja occidentalis, 35
    plicata, 35
Thuja, 35
Tilia americana, 70
Toxicodendron vernix, 127
Toyon, 121
Tree-of-heaven, 102
Tremella mesenterica, 259
Tricholoma flavovirens, 222
    portentosum, 222
    vaccinum, 223
Tricholoma, 213-214, 222-223
    Dingy, 222
    Greenish-yellow, 222
    Maroon, 214
    Russet-scaly, 223
Tricholomopsis rutilans, 214
Trichomanes boschianum, 144

Tripe, Rock, 194
Truffle, False, 257
Tsuga canadensis, 12
    caroliniana, 12
    heterophylla, 12
    mertensiana, 12
Tuliptree, Chinese, 41
Tupelo, 93
    Black, 93
    Water, 93
Tylopilus felleus, 246

Ulmus alata, 49
    americana, 48
    rubra, 48
Ulotrichales, 183
Ulva lactuca, 183
Umbellularia californica, 42
Umbilicaria papulosa, 194
Urnula craterium, 263
Usnea cavernosa, 195

Vaccinium angustifolium, 118
    arboreum, 118
    corymbosum, 118
Verpa bohemica, 268
Viburnum alnifolium, 129
    lentago, 129
Viburnum, 129
Volvaria, Silky, 224
Volvariella bombycina, 224

Wahoo (shrub), 125
Wahoo (tree), 49
Walnut, 50-51
    Black, 51
    English, 50
    White, 51
Waterlocust, 90
Waterwort, Fringed, 181
Waxmyrtle, 111
White-cedar, 36

Atlantic, 36
    Northern, 35
    Southern, 36
White-mangrove, 91
Willow, 71
    Black, 73
    Desert-, 108
    Peachleaf, 72
    Pussy (Glaucous), 72
    Sandbar, 71
    Weeping, 73
Winterberry, Common, 92
Witches' Butter, 259
    Black, 260
Witch-hazel, 109
Woodlover, Smoky-gilled, 228
Woodsia ilvensis, 156
    obtusa, 156
    oregana, 157
    scopulina, 157
Woodsia, Blunt-lobed, 156
    Mountain, 157
    Rusty, 156
    Western, 157
Woodwardia areolata, 164
    fimbriata, 165
    virginica, 164

Xanthoria elegans, 193
Xeromphalina campanella, 215
Xylaria polymorpha, 261

Yaupon, 92
Yellow-poplar, 41
Yew, 13
    Canada, 13
    Pacific, 13
Yucca brevifolia, 108
Yucca, 108

Zanthoxylum americanum, 103
    clava-herculis, 103

Credits and acknowledgments for the original edition of North American Wildlife

Staff
Editor: Susan J. Wernert
Art Editor: Richard J. Berenson
Associate Editors: James Dwyer,
    Sally French
Designers: Ken Chaya,
    Larissa Lawrynenko
Contributing Editor:
    Katharine R. O'Hare
Contributing Copy Editor:
    Patricia M. Godfrey

Consulting Editor
Durward L. Allen
    Professor of Wildlife Ecology
Department of Forestry and
Natural Resources
Purdue University

Consultants
John W. Andresen
    Director, Urban Forestry
    Studies Programme
University of Toronto

Howard E. Bigelow
    Professor of Botany
University of Massachusetts

Howard Crum
    Professor of Botany
Warren Herb Wagner, Jr.
    Professor of Botany
The University of Michigan

Thomas H. Everett
    Senior Horticulture Specialist
John T. Michel
    Senior Curator of Ferns
The New York Botanical Garden

John M. Kingsbury
    Professor of Botany
Cornell University

Alton A. Lindsey
    Emeritus Professor of Ecology
Purdue University

D. Bruce Means
    Director, Tall Timbers
    Research Station

Richard Mitchell
    State Botanist of New York
Charles J. Sheviak
    Curator of Botany
New York State Museum

Contributing Artists
Dorothea Barlowe; George Buctel;
Eva Cellini; Ken Chaya; John D.
Dawson; Mary Kellner; Elizabeth
McClelland; Wayne Trimm